Fundamentals of Negotiation

Fundamentals of Negotiation

A Guide for Environmental Professionals

Jeffrey G. Miller Thomas R. Colosi

Environmental Law Institute
Washington, D.C.

Published 1989. Sixth printing April 1999.

Printed in the United States of America

ISBN 0-911937-28-5

Library of Congress Cataloging-in-Publication Data

Miller, Jeffrey, G., 1941-
Fundamentals of negotiation.

(An ELI monograph)
Bibliography: p.
1. Environmental mediation—United States. I. Colosi, Thomas R. II. Title. III. Series: ELI monograph series (Unnumbered)
KF3775.M56 1989 344.73 '046 89-11937
ISBN 0-911937-28-5 347.30446

Contents

Figures

All figures and related text are derived from COLLECTIVE BARGAINING: HOW IT WORKS AND WHY, *by Thomas Colosi and Arthur Eliot Berkeley (1986). Adapted by permission of the publisher, the American Arbitration Association, 140 West 51st Street, New York, New York 10020.*

Foreword

The art of settlement is no less important to the lawyer than the art of advocacy. Indeed, the main purpose of the trial calendar is to notify adversaries that the time for settlement is at hand. About 95 percent of the federal civil cases filed each year settle before trial. In 1987, for example, 11,913 federal civil cases went to trial, while 225,569 were settled. In state courts, the percentages are even more dramatic. In New York in 1988, for example, more than 97 percent of cases settled. And these are percentages of cases actually *filed*; they do not take into account the disputes in which lawyers negotiated settlements that made filings unnecessary.

Yet the legal literature focuses on the adversary process. Relatively few materials, particularly in the environmental field, are designed to help lawyers hone basic negotiating skills. *Fundamentals of Negotiation: A Guide for Environmental Professionals* seeks to fill that gap.

ELI's 20 years of experience in providing environmental professionals with legal and technical training on a wide range of environmental law and policy topics have made us acutely aware of the need for a book like this. Long before dispute resolution became a standard term in the environmental policy vocabulary, ELI was deeply involved in understanding and promoting efforts to resolve environmental disputes. Since 1979, ELI and the American Arbitration Association have conducted a nationwide training program that has presented more than 50 environmental negotiation courses to the Environmental Protection Agency, state agencies, and the private bar.

This ongoing series of courses is based on the premise that negotiation, like other skills, can be developed but must be practiced. The courses both teach basic negotiation skills through lectures and build those skills through role-playing exercises simulating actual enforcement and regulatory disputes. This short book cannot encompass the richness of the training program, but it captures the essence of the teaching and draws on examples and recurring fact situations encountered by course participants.

To create this handbook, ELI called on Thomas Colosi and Jeffrey Miller, the stars of our negotiation training courses. Thomas Colosi is Vice President for National Affairs of the American Arbitration Association. He is an experienced negotiator who has conducted negotiation training for many organizations, including EPA, the Foreign Service Institute, and private firms. He has taught courses on negotiation and alternative methods of dispute resolution at various universities and government agencies, and has trained negotiators all over the world. Jeffrey Miller, now a law professor at Pace University School of Law, was an enforcement officer at EPA for 10 years, serving as Director of the Enforcement Division and Chief of the Enforcement Branch in Region I, and then directing the entire EPA enforcement program as Assistant Administrator. He has also practiced law, most recently with Perkins Coie, and previously with Bergson, Borkland, Margolis & Adler and Verner, Liipfert, Bernhard, McPherson & Hand in Washington, D.C. He has represented both citizen and industry interests in environmental disputes and has extensive experience in conducting environmental negotiations.

This handbook stresses the unique aspects of negotiating environmental disputes. These disputes tend to be extraordinarily complex because they frequently involve difficult scientific and economic issues as well as numerous governmental and private parties; the authors coin the term "hydraheaded" to describe these complex multi-party proceedings. Noting also that many environmental disputes are highly politicized and that their public nature invites grandstanding, the authors write,

> In short, it's a wonder that some environmental disputes are ever settled. To achieve settlements that the parties are comfortable with and that will wear well over time, environmental negotiators need special ability to deal with complexity and ambiguity, high tolerance for vilification, and great patience and perseverance. Thorough mastery of the negotiating process therefore is especially helpful in negotiating environmental disputes.

The authors stress the importance of actively *managing* environmental negotiations. They first outline the underlying principles of negotiation, then graphically illustrate the need for management by describing a hypothetical, but unnervingly plausible, *unmanaged* negotiation. Subsequent chapters on the fundamentals of preparing for and conducting negotiations, on communication, and on management of personnel and policy changes give practical advice that will be invaluable to beginning environmental attorneys and welcome to others who seek to improve their skills.

As a national non-profit research, education, and publishing organization dedicated to the development of more effective and more efficient environmental protection and pollution control programs, the Environmental Law Institute takes pride in publication of this book. Our publications and educational programs will continue to develop and promote improved environmental dispute resolution. We think *Fundamentals of Negotiation: A Guide for Environmental Professionals* will help achieve this goal, and will prove to be an invaluable shelfmate to ELI's other reference works.

—J. William Futrell, President
Environmental Law Institute

Chapter 1: Introduction

Learning About Negotiation

We are all capable of becoming better negotiators. The question is, how can we do it? For the most part, we are left to our own devices to discover how to negotiate effectively. Few schools teach negotiation, and many popular books on the subject contain as much hype as anything else. Most of us therefore develop our negotiating skills based on what we learn from the many negotiations we conduct every day. We learn from those we negotiate with and against, and we learn from our own mistakes and successes. Like any other skill, negotiating comes more naturally to some than to others, and we all bring to it our individual experiences, strengths, and weaknesses. But apart from instinct and practice, are there specific techniques that will improve negotiating skills? Can they be learned from a monograph such as this one?

Negotiation, like litigation, is a process, not a science. Learning to negotiate is problematic because the process is complex and has few hard and fast rules. Much of the complexity arises from the infinite variety among negotiators and negotiating situations. Indeed, every negotiation develops a life of its own based on the nature and number of the issues, the character and strengths of the parties, and the negotiating skills of the players. Because there is no rule book and success depends on the dynamics of each individual negotiation, much of the negotiating process can be learned only through practice. You can't become a skilled negotiator merely by reading.

Nevertheless, there are fundamental techniques and concepts that can be useful in many different negotiating situations. A book can help negotiators learn these techniques and concepts. To that end, this monograph:

- suggests a conceptual framework for understanding the negotiation process that gives some order to an otherwise apparently unstructured situation;
- elucidates the few "rules" that do exist; and
- explains the nature, usefulness, and limitations of a number of techniques employed by experienced and successful negotiators.

This monograph grew out of more than three dozen environmental negotiation courses presented by the authors around the country. The courses included both lectures on the negotiation process and practice sessions in which participants negotiated environmental disputes, then discussed these negotiations with faculty observers. Such managed practice affords the optimum opportunity for skills development.

The monograph captures much of the message of the courses. It is oriented toward the problems that course participants identified as common to environmental disputes and to their jobs. Although it cannot duplicate the learning opportunity of the practice negotiations, it benefits from the authors' observations of those negotiations. Many of the examples used in the monograph are drawn directly from these observations.

Negotiating Environmental Disputes

Is negotiating an environmental dispute different from negotiating any other type of dispute? In one sense, no. The basic negotiating process and skills are much the same no matter what is being negotiated. A skilled negotiator can operate effectively in many substantive areas if assisted by expert advisors. Thus George Shultz easily moved from negotiating domestic labor-management disputes as Secretary of Labor to negotiating international political disputes as Secretary of State.

In another sense, however, negotiating an environmental dispute may be different: Environmental disputes can be extraordinarily complex and visible. The complexities can involve both multiple substantive issues and multiple parties. Substantively, a single dispute can pose questions of science, engineering, economics, law, politics, and public acceptance, and may present difficult problems in each of these fields. Many branches of science and engineering may be relevant, and the disputed issues may be at the cutting edges of the disciplines, where there is little or no hard knowledge and much disagreement. Economic impacts can be local or national, mild or severe, predictable or conjectural. Environmental law is complex, fast-changing, and fraught with unanswered questions. Many environmental disputes also become political issues of local, state, or national interest. Politics may even make them unresolvable. Finally, environmental issues may be of great interest to a locally affected public, a particular public interest sector, or the public at large. Resolution without public acceptance will be difficult.

Environmental disputes also can involve multiple parties, including governments, public interest groups, private companies, and private individuals; often there are many parties in each category. A single Superfund case can involve several hundred individual, corporate, and governmental defendants, as well as more than one governmental plaintiff. Even a single governmental party can be a hydraheaded monster. The Environmental Protection Agency (EPA), for example, may be at war within itself on several different planes. EPA and its attorney, the Department of Justice (DOJ), may not see eye to eye. The DOJ in Washington and the local U.S. Attorney may be in disagreement. State parties may be just as fractured and also may have different views than federal parties. Finally, private parties may well be divided within and among themselves.

As if these complexities weren't enough, the public nature of many environmental disputes means that they are negotiated in a fishbowl—the atmosphere least conducive to successful negotiation. Publicity encourages negotiators to play to public audiences rather than to deal realistically with their counterparts. It invites grandstanding and the taking of extreme positions that become hard to modify.

In short, it's a wonder that some environmental disputes are ever settled. To achieve settlements that the parties are comfortable with and that will wear well over time, environmental negotiators need special ability to deal with complexity and ambiguity, high tolerance for vilification, and great patience and perseverance. Thorough mastery of the negotiating process therefore is especially helpful in negotiating environmental disputes. This command of the basics gives the negotiator running room to deal with all the complexities and uncertainties inherent in these disputes.

Organization of Monograph

Chapter Two of this monograph outlines some principles underlying the negotiation process. Chapter Three presents the Case of the Unmanaged Negotiation. This sterling example of how *not* to negotiate an environmental dispute will illustrate many of the points made later. Chapter Four articulates the main theme of the monograph—that environmental negotiations must be managed—and explains the fundamentals of managing them. Chapter Five addresses ways to communicate effectively in negotiations. Chapter Six discusses how to deal with the common problem of policy and personnel changes during negotiations. Chapter Seven summarizes the major lessons of the monograph.

Reading, studying, and assimilating this monograph won't make you an expert negotiator. But it will make you aware of many ways in which you can negotiate better. If you practice them and make them your own, you will be well on your way to becoming a skilled negotiator.

Chapter 2: Understanding Negotiation

A successful negotiator must understand the nature of the negotiation process. This chapter discusses some of the fundamentals of that process.

The Importance of Trust

By telling you in Chapter One that you can't learn to negotiate from this monograph alone, we accomplished an objective that is essential to negotiation. We told you the truth as we understand it, hopefully establishing trust.

Settlement is unlikely unless the negotiating teams develop some degree of trust. The Secretary General of the United Nations underscored this point recently by commenting that the first week of his mediation between Iraq and Iran resulted in no progress because neither side trusted the other. Settlements are basically exchanges of promises—enforceable promises when reduced to contracts or consent orders, but promises nonetheless. And you don't willingly exchange promises with people you don't trust. A regulatory agency may be less reluctant to enter into a consent decree with a party it does not wholly trust, because it knows a court will enforce compliance. Even in a regulatory negotiation, however, each side wants the other to listen to it, to understand its needs, and to modify its own positions accordingly. All this is more likely if the parties trust one another.

The importance of trust extends well beyond the negotiation at hand and the implementation of its settlement. A negotiator's reputation for trustworthiness or untrustworthiness will follow him or her from one negotiation to the next, making future negotiations easier or more difficult, and thus making the negotiator more or less valuable to prospective clients.

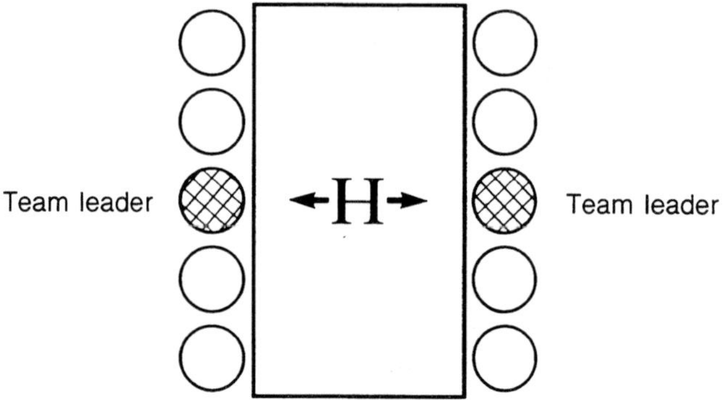

Figure 1: Horizontal (H) bargaining

The Importance of Identifying All the Dimensions of Negotiations

To negotiate effectively, you must identify all the bargaining configurations within your negotiation. A negotiating team bargains not only with its opposite number across the table, but also within itself and with its client's hierarchy (the chain of command through which the negotiators report and which ultimately must be satisfied with and sign off on the negotiators' results). You must gain the trust, understand the objectives, and manage the behavior of all these elements. While this may sound like a complicated set of negotiations for your side, the other side's situation is similarly complex. (*See infra* pp. 23-31.) You may find it helpful to examine your particular negotiation in terms of the following three basic bargaining configurations, which appear in all complex negotiations.

Horizontal Bargaining

The average negotiation appears to feature only one bargaining configuration: across-the-table, or horizontal, bargaining. (See Figure 1.) Although it may look like a good deal of bargaining occurs in this formalized configuration, this may be deceptive. In fact, in difficult negotiations, very little actual bargaining occurs across the table. The activities that do occur there are by no means unimportant, however, because they may set the tone for future negotiation. These activities may include information sharing, posturing, educating, orating, yelling, cursing, begging, wheedling, crying, threatening, emotional grandstanding, etc.

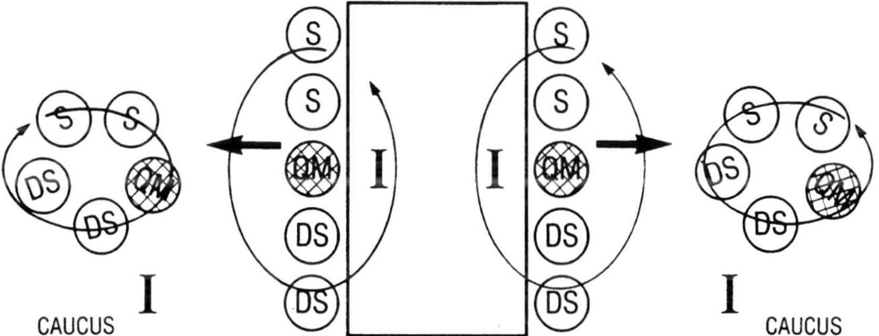

Figure 2: Internal (I) bargaining. "S" stands for "stabilizer," "DS" for "destabilizer," and "QM" for "quasi-mediator"; *see infra* pp. 19-20

Internal Bargaining

Where then does most of the *real* bargaining take place? Within each team, away from the table, in caucus. (See Figure 2.) Each team constantly conducts active internal negotiations to decide whether, when, how, how far, and in what direction it will move; what promises it will make; etc. (*See infra* pp. 23-25.)

Vertical Bargaining

Each team must bargain not only within itself, but also with its client's hierarchy and other constituencies. (See Figure 3.) Because each interested party may have numerous constituencies with different interests, this configuration is also called "constituencies bargaining." Vertical bargaining also takes place within the client's hierarchy.

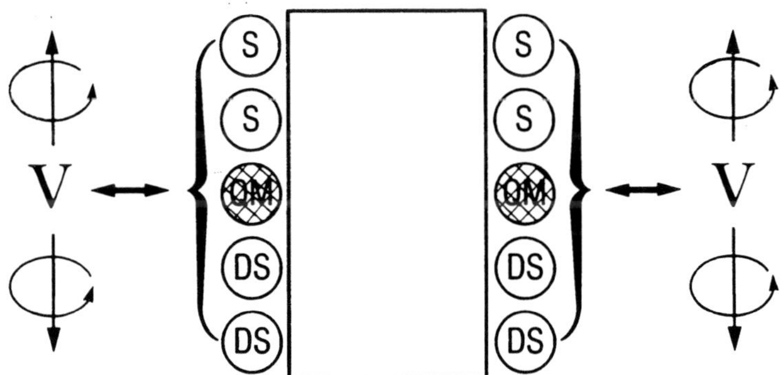

Figure 3: Vertical (V) bargaining

Some Advantages of Negotiation

Negotiation frequently offers great advantages over administrative or judicial litigation or other dispute resolution procedures with third-party decisionmakers. Negotiation may be quicker and less resource-intensive. It also lets parties devise solutions tailored to their needs and situations. Any solution it results in has been agreed to by both parties. Both sides should be happy with the solution, or at least able to live with it comfortably. And parties are more likely to ratify, and comply ungrudgingly and completely with, a solution they have agreed to than one imposed by others without their consent. Because the parties have agreed to the solution, they have a stake in the success of its implementation.

Reaching the Best Settlement

Because each negotiation takes on a life of its own, no two sets of negotiators are likely to reach the same settlement on a matter of any complexity. In negotiation courses taught by the authors, for example, participants have consistently reached different settlements of the same practice problems. This suggests that many disputes may have no "right" settlement. From each side's perspective, however, there may well be a range in the desirability of various settlements. The existence of a range of acceptable settlements rather than a single "right" settlement may disturb the less flexible or the advocate of narrow interests, but it expands the opportunities available to the skilled negotiator.

In a normal settlement, neither side gets all that it had hoped for when negotiations began. This does not mean that either side "sold out" on what it did not achieve. A party may learn during the course of negotiations that its original expectations were unwarranted or ill-founded. It may trade less desired items to get more desired items. It may forego unnecessary items to secure agreement. But it should not give up what it considers essential. In some cases, a party may be able to accept only one solution to a problem. In such cases, negotiation and settlement are irrelevant—the solution is simply non-negotiable.

To reach a settlement, all parties must have their needs met to some degree. This may not always be possible if the parties insist on following models developed to resolve other disputes or on adhering to the original nomenclature of their own dispute. Creativity in recasting proposals, issues, or settlements and flexibility in accepting new concepts or words will help resolve some negotiations.

The Interaction of Negotiation and Litigation

Parties sometimes threaten to sue each other unless a settlement is negotiated by a certain date. To some this suggests that negotiation and litigation are mutually exclusive processes. Nothing could be farther from the truth. Approximately 80 percent of all cases filed in court settle through negotiation before trial on the merits. Aspects of the litigation process facilitate the negotiation of settlements. For example, discovery helps get all the relevant facts on the table. Motion practice can be used to speed or slow the pace of a negotiation to the benefit of the moving party. Resolution of legal issues by motion can also reopen negotiations previously deadlocked over those issues. In addition, court-imposed deadlines can stimulate closure. Conversely, some aspects of litigation, such as its adversarial (win/lose) nature, hinder negotiation. Therefore, negotiation and litigation are not mutually exclusive processes for settling disputes. Negotiation not only precedes the onset of litigation but continues during and after the commencement of litigation and sometimes even after adjudication. It simply follows different ground rules in each phase.

Chapter 3: The Case of the Unmanaged Negotiation

The key theme of this monograph is that negotiations can and must be managed. (*See* Chapter 4.) The following case study shows some of the ways that negotiations can be *un*managed, as well as some of the consequences.

This case is an amalgam of several situations observed by the authors in actual negotiations and described to them by training course participants. Although it involves a negotiation between governmental and private parties, it could just as well involve two governmental or two private parties.

Sam Acosta has just become acting Chief of the Resource Conservation and Recovery Act (RCRA) Enforcement Section in an EPA Regional Office. Until now he has been in the RCRA State Program Section. He finds on his desk a short action memorandum from Bill Sanders, a RCRA inspector. The memorandum recommends issuing an administrative order to a hazardous waste treatment facility called Treatment Supreme ("TS") for violations of interim authorization security and manifest requirements. Sanders writes that during an inspection he observed a 25-foot gap in the fence at the back of the TS facility. He also states that TS failed to note discrepancies on manifests for 75 shipments of one waste stream, when the analysis performed by TS did not confirm that the waste was as represented by the generator. Sanders attaches a copy of a draft administrative order requiring restoration of the fence, prohibiting further receipts of the waste stream, and assessing a $25,000 penalty. He notes that copies of the manifests and laboratory reports are in the inspection file. Sanders is no longer in the office. He is working for the state for a year on a rotational assignment.

Sam signs off on the action memorandum and sends it to his boss. It is eventually sent to the Regional Counsel's office for legal review, and is assigned to Laura Smith. Laura's main job at EPA has been handling the legal aspects of sewage treatment facility construction grants. This is her first experience with RCRA and her first enforcement case. She is instructed that the RCRA office is responsible for substantive determinations and that her role is to assure that the order is legally sustainable, to assist the RCRA office in any resulting negotiations, and to represent that office in any subsequent appeals. She reviews the order and action memorandum and determines that the violations alleged are supported by the action memorandum and are sufficient to justify the remedies sought. She compares the draft order with agency guidance and makes some changes to conform it to the guidance. She signs off on the order and it is eventually issued.

Guy Larado, outside attorney for TS, calls Laura to request a conference on the order, hopefully to negotiate a mutually acceptable resolution. She indicates she must check Sam's calendar and they arrange three possible times, depending on Sam's availability. She calls Sam, settles on a date three weeks hence, and arranges to meet with Sam that afternoon to review the case.

When Laura and Sam meet they review the action memorandum and order. Laura asks to see copies of Sanders' inspection report and the manifests. She asks whether they can talk to Sanders, but Sam says he has been assigned to the state for a year. They agree that the case seems open and shut and that under EPA's penalty guidance they can only agree to mitigate the penalty down to $18,000. They agree that Laura will be the spokesperson in the negotiations. They tell both of their superiors that they intend to settle for the substantive relief set forth in the order and a penalty between $18,000 and $25,000. Their superiors concur.

As the meeting date approaches, Laura attempts to meet with Sam again, but they are both out of the office much of the time and do not connect. The day before the meeting she attempts to arrange for a conference room, but all of them are already claimed. Instead she arranges to meet in Sam's office, which is larger than hers.

On the day of the meeting Laura goes to Sam's office five minutes early, telling the main receptionist to ring her there when Larado and TS arrive. Larado, however, is familiar with the EPA offices and proceeds directly to Laura's office, never coming near the main receptionist. Laura's secretary is not there and no one knows where she is. Both negotiating teams remain in splendid isolation until Laura's secretary returns, discovers the situation, and calls Laura.

Laura returns to her office, meets the TS contingent, and escorts them to Sam's office. There are six of them: TS's plant manager, chief chemist, in-house attorney, and outside attorney, and its customer's plant manager and attorney. There are only four chairs in Sam's office. Sam and Laura scurry around to find more chairs. Sam sits behind the desk, Laura sits beside it, and the TS contingent crowds in front of it, filling all the space between it and the door. The room is not large enough to hold them all comfortably.

Laura opens by introducing herself and Sam and inviting the TS representatives to introduce themselves. She apologizes for the confusion and for the cramped quarters. She then outlines the Agency's view of the importance and gravity of the violations and states that it would like to see if there is a basis for settling the matter. She indicates that the substantive violations must be corrected expeditiously. Finally, she says, "We really would like to get a penalty of around $18,000 to $20,000."

Guy Larado responds with a statement that TS explained both alleged violations to the EPA inspector when he was on site and that it believes the order is a mistake. He asks whether the inspector is coming to the meeting. Sam says the inspector has been assigned to the state and is not available. Larado says that is a pity, since TS has already been through this with the inspector.

As to the fence, Larado says, there was indeed a 25-foot section missing the day the inspector was there. It was missing as the result of an automobile accident on the adjoining highway. It was scheduled for repair within the week and was in fact repaired two days later. Incidentally, it was a 10-foot-high, electrified, chain link fence topped with concertina wire, which was far more protective than was required or was customary in the trade. Larado produced pictures of the fence, a notarized affidavit from the repair company as to when it was repaired, and a copy of a letter to the inspector enclosing copies of the pictures and affidavit. Sam said that satisfied him that the violation had been corrected. Laura said that there was still a question of the penalty. Larado said that a penalty might be legally authorized, but that equitably it should be mitigated to zero because the hole in the fence had been caused by a third party beyond TS's control, TS had scheduled the repair before the inspection and had completed it immediately thereafter, and the fence was far better than EPA's regulations required. Sam said, "I hear you. Let's talk about the manifest violations."

Larado said TS had discussed those with the inspector too. The waste stream in question was being delisted when the inspection took place and subsequently was delisted, so it wasn't a hazardous waste at all. TS's customer confirmed this and produced a copy of the delisting decision and accompanying Federal Register notice. Larado said that TS had sent the inspector a letter explaining this and enclosing a copy of the delisting document and notice. Laura asked Sam if copies of TS's letters to the inspector were in his file, for they weren't in hers. He said he didn't know, but looked through his file and found both letters.

Larado said TS could argue that by delisting the waste stream, EPA acknowledged that it was never really hazardous waste, and therefore that TS never really violated the manifest requirements. He said TS would forego that argument for the sake of settlement if EPA would acknowledge that the waste stream was not hazardous, and therefore that the violations were technical, no damage was done to the environment or the regulatory scheme, and a de minimis penalty, if any, was appropriate. He offered $2500. Sam said that sounded fine to him, but the violations raised questions about the integrity of TS's manifest handling system and waste analysis plan. Larado answered that EPA's inspector had found no other problems, but that TS would hire an outside auditor to review its system and would follow the auditor's recommendations if defects were found. Sam asked if TS would agree to put that in a consent order, and Larado said it would.

Larado said that there appeared to be agreement: they would settle on a $2500 penalty and an agreement to audit TS's manifest system and correct any deficiencies. At this point Laura said she thought EPA's penalty policy would require more than $2500 for the admitted violations. Larado said Sam had already agreed to $2500. Sam said he hadn't agreed to the figure, only that under the facts a relatively low penalty seemed appropriate. Larado asked how much, and Sam asked Laura if she thought $5000 would be enough. She said she didn't know. Larado said TS would write a check for $4000 and deliver it that day to settle the matter. Sam said he didn't see how a settlement could be done so quickly, since it had to be signed off higher up, which usually took at least two weeks.

Larado, who up to this point had been soft-spoken, polite, and charming, became red in the face and began speaking in a louder voice, touched with anger. He protested that he had spoken at length with the inspector about the importance of a quick resolution of the matter. TS was about to close a major financing to construct three new state-of-the-art incinerators in an EPA Region to the east and had to certify a clean regulatory bill of health to secure the financing. Larado said the inspector had assured him that if TS could reach a settlement with EPA's negotiators, the resulting paperwork could be handled in a couple of days. Larado said he was dumbfounded that

EPA would hold up so important a matter over violations that it agreed were trivial and of no consequence.

Sam asked Laura whether she saw any reason not to agree to the settlement outlined. She said she hadn't really seen enough of these problems to be sure. Sam said as far as he was concerned the violations, as explained, were technical, the solutions were adequate, and the penalty was appropriate. Laura said he was the client and she was satisfied if he was. Larado then drew up a letter agreement. Both parties initialed it, and Laura agreed to convert it into a consent order that afternoon.

That afternoon Laura talked to Sanders, the inspector, by phone. He confirmed that he had indicated that quick action was possible if agreement was reached, but said that this agreement was inappropriate. The fence break had indeed been caused by an automobile accident and had been repaired immediately after the inspection. But the break had occurred four months previously and TS had not ordered the repair until it knew an inspection was scheduled. The fence was indeed far better than those around most disposal facilities. But the state had ordered TS to install it after previous fencing had proven inadequate to prevent repeated damage by vandals. TS was correct that the waste stream involved in the manifest violations was later delisted. But the real question was whether the shipments received really were of that waste stream or whether TS had been accepting a nonpermitted waste. Indeed, Sanders wondered whether he hadn't made a mistake in not recommending action against TS's customer for sending a waste to a disposal facility not permitted to take it. He was surprised Laura didn't know this because most of it was in his handwritten notes, which he was sure were in the file somewhere.

At this point, EPA's negotiating team recognized that it was in an embarrassing situation.

Chapter 4: Managing Negotiations

Negotiation is a process or system designed for resolving disputes and planning future activities. Like any process or system, it has little chance of success unless it is managed. Appreciating this point is a giant step toward improving negotiating performance. Management responsibilities fall primarily on negotiating team leaders, but all participants must cooperate for management to be effective.

Management tasks fall into several rough and overlapping categories, including management of information, behavior, time, process, and expectations. One element common to all these categories is the overwhelming necessity for preparation.

Preparation

Importance of Preparation

If any single element is the key to successful negotiation, it is preparation. An unprepared negotiating team will rarely achieve as satisfactory a result as a prepared team. Indeed, an unprepared team can achieve a settlement so unsatisfactory that its client will or should reject it. Yet many negotiators skimp on preparation.

In the Case of the Unmanaged Negotiation (Chapter 3), all the EPA team's failings can be traced to inadequate preparation. This team was unprepared in all respects. As a threshold matter, little thought was given to team composition or structure. Laura was simply thrust into the case, and the team didn't really have a leader.

The EPA team also was blind to the real facts of its case. (For a discussion of facts and "facts" in negotiations, *see infra* pp. 46-47.) All the necessary information was available for it to arrive at a completely different, and far more favorable, settlement. In this regard, the lack of one preparatory meeting with or phone call to the inspector obviously spelled disaster. Indeed, the team hadn't even reviewed all the information in its own files. The inspector's undiscovered notes would have alerted it to the necessity of talking to the inspector and to the true seriousness of the violations. Failure to obtain this information meant that the team could not begin to assess the strengths and weaknesses of its case. Less obvious are the consequences of the team's failure to discover from the EPA Region to the east that TS was in the process of getting permits and money to construct RCRA incinerators and needed an environmental bill of good health. This knowledge could have given the EPA team leverage to extract what it wanted as the price of that bill of good health. Instead, the information was used against it.

The EPA team also lacked informed and agreed-upon objectives and strategies, as well as internal discipline and rules for conducting the negotiation. The latter deficiency became evident when Sam would not allow Laura to be their spokesperson despite their prior agreement that she would be; when Laura acquiesced in Sam's actions; and when Sam and Laura openly caucused between themselves on several issues right before the eyes and ears of TS, thus enabling Larado to take control of the meeting and side with Sam to divide and conquer Sam and Laura.

Finally, lack of proper logistical preparation led to a mix-up on where TS was to meet the EPA team and to cramped, inappropriate negotiating quarters. This embarrassed Laura and probably made the EPA team prone to making a compensatory gesture to TS. The crowd of TS team members separating Sam and Laura from the door probably also inhibited them from leaving the room to caucus.

In contrast to the EPA team, the TS team was reasonably well-prepared. It included all the necessary personnel, it knew the facts of its case well, and it had clearly decided in advance what it wanted and what approach it would take. The team was not ideally prepared; for example, it should have found out in advance what EPA personnel would be at the meeting, since the inspector's presence would have required it to use a different strategy. However, the team's strong factual knowledge, clear objectives, and tight internal discipline enabled it to adapt its behavior to take full advantage of each weakness that the EPA team displayed.

Constituting and Characterizing the Negotiating Team

Before a team can manage or be managed, it must be constituted. In choosing team members, bear in mind that their number, experience, and personalities must be suited to the negotiation at hand, and that they must be able to work together. Moreover, at least one team member should be well acquainted with each major legal and technical area likely to be subject to negotiation. It is frequently useful for one team member to be a "numbers" person or statistician, and other team members should have appropriate technical expertise. The team should also be able to draw on others, as needed, for expertise on particular issues.

Every negotiating team needs a leader. The team leader may be designated by the client or agreed on by the team. The leader bears the brunt of responsibility for assuring that the team is well prepared and, if necessary, for negotiating with the client's hierarchy for the time and resources necessary for proper preparation. The leader should be adept at process, skilled in oral communication, and capable of managing negotiations. He or she should also be a keen observer of behavior and an excellent listener. The leader need not necessarily have substantive expertise, although the team is much better off if he or she does. Attorneys are often designated as team leaders because they are trained in verbal skills and are often adept at understanding process. Non-attorneys can also make excellent team leaders. More sophisticated teams in complicated cases may designate one person as team chairperson and another as chief spokesperson.

Other team roles also need to be filled. For example, one team member should take complete notes during each negotiating session and should serve as a listener and observer. This person notes not only what is said, but what body language and inflection accompany the spoken words, and what reaction those words elicit from each team.

Apart from their formal assigned roles, team members will naturally fall into certain generic roles based on their personalities and interests. Most negotiating teams include at least three types of members: stabilizers, destabilizers, and quasi-mediators. (See Figure 4.) These types may have very different interests. However, members' roles can and often do change during the negotiation process, and may vary from issue to issue. On certain issues, all members may be stabilizers or destabilizers.

Stabilizers are committed to the negotiation process and oriented toward reaching agreement, sometimes at any cost. In internal team negotiations, stabilizers tend to encourage movement toward settlement. If a team leader is a stabilizer, the team may settle too quickly and easily.

Destabilizers may lack commitment to the negotiation process, feel more comfortable with self-help or litigation techniques, behave disruptively, and be unwilling to settle at any price. In internal team negotiations, destabilizers tend to resist movement toward settlement.

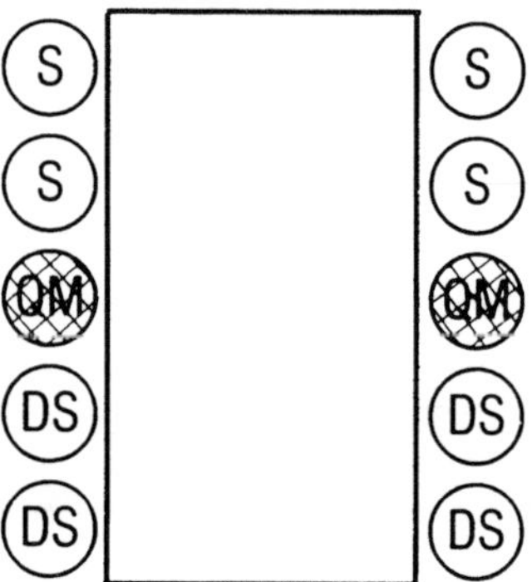

Figure 4: Types of team members—stabilizers (S), destabilizers (DS), and quasi-mediators (QM)

If a team leader is a destabilizer, the team is less likely to agree to settlement, even on reasonable terms.

Quasi-mediators, who are usually the chief negotiators, are committed to the negotiation process and to the achievement of workable settlements that are acceptable to both sides. In internal team negotiations, quasi-mediators seek to harmonize the interests of the stabilizers, who may concede too readily, and the destabilizers, who may adhere to impractical positions. They also seek to facilitate and implement decisions and to keep the team unified. Although clearly advocates, they are often allied with any outside neutrals, such as mediators. Team leaders usually are—or should be—quasi-mediators.

Preparing the Team

The basic work of managing the negotiating team and its client must be done at the preparation stage. After the team members are chosen and their roles designated, the team should formulate ground rules for its conduct. These include, for example, rules on when and how to caucus; on who can speak at the negotiating table; and on how to resolve internal disputes. (*See infra* pp. 23-25.) The team should also work (or negotiate) with the client's hierarchy to obtain needed support, agree on the objectives of the negotiation, and establish an ongoing line of communication. (*See infra* pp. 26-28.)

☐ *Substantive Preparation.* Substantive preparation is critical. It begins with research identifying the relevant facts and laws and determining what, if any, additional facts and laws must be learned and legal considerations explored before the negotiation commences or concludes. The team must determine whether the other side can provide needed facts (and, if so, whether its information will be reliable), or whether the team must gather the facts independently. Each issue to be negotiated must then be identified, together with its importance to the client and the range of resolutions to it that the client can accept. Issues on which flexibility and compromise are easiest should be identified. Finally, the strengths and weaknesses of the client's case must be analyzed and their implications understood.

☐ *Investigating the Opposition.* Basic intelligence information must be gathered on the opposition and its negotiating team. Who will be sitting across the table? The team should obtain as much information as possible about its opposition, including answers to the following questions:

- How powerful is it?
- How is it structured?
- How trustworthy is it?
- How cooperative or litigious is it?
- To what pressures is it susceptible?
- What leverage (e.g., enforcement tools, adverse publicity, positive incentives) does the client have over it, and how can the client use that leverage?
- Can the client meaningfully interfere with its plans (e.g., to secure a loan, sell an issue of stock, receive favorable publicity, consummate a merger)?
- What facts does it have?
- What facts must it make known before the negotiation can be concluded?
- Which of its assertions are based on facts and which on assumptions?
- What issues does it see and how important does it consider them?
- What are its expectations and how can they be lowered?
- What are its underlying needs, interests, and assumptions?
- What is its likely opening position?
- How will it react to various possible demands?
- What are the strengths and weaknesses of its case, and how can they be exploited?

The team should learn as much about the other negotiating team as about the opposing party itself. Useful questions include:

- Who are the team members?
- What are their backgrounds?
- What team roles do they play?

- What are their negotiating styles?
- How disciplined are they?
- How sophisticated are they in negotiation?
- What weaknesses can you use to your advantage?
- What strengths must you anticipate and prepare for?
- How sophisticated are they in the use of mediation, arbitration, and litigation?
- Are they trustworthy?
- How do they relate to their client's hierarchy?

Intelligence information on the other side can be gathered from many places: business literature, the news media, SEC filings, EPA and other government agency records, etc. Intelligence information should be gathered orally as well, particularly on the other side's negotiators. If the opposing party is well known, others will have dealt with its representatives, and they will usually tell you about them if asked.

Moving Into the Negotiation

Now, and only now, is the team in a position to refine its objectives, formulate a strategy to reach those objectives, and develop an opening position or offer and appropriate fallbacks or alternatives. At this stage it is also ready to draft an agenda and determine what logistical arrangements best suit its interests. After these steps are completed, the team leader should contact the other team's leader to discuss the agenda and logistics. Information should also be exchanged on team size and composition. If there are significant disparities, the team leader may wish to alter the team's size or composition or negotiate with the other side for a mutual limitation. The team should also research the characteristics and negotiating styles of any unfamiliar members of the other team.

At this point, preparation with the other team begins. This preparation may continue through the commencement of the first negotiating session, when the teams should agree on an agenda and negotiating rules.

The agenda, which may cover both the initial negotiating session and subsequent sessions, is important in a number of respects. It should surface all the issues and make it hard to raise last-minute concerns. It should order the proceedings advantageously. For example, it could start with the more easily resolved issues, thus building good feelings, commitment to the process, and momentum toward settlement. The agenda can also set deadlines for completing different aspects of the negotiation.

The teams should also agree at this point on basic rules governing the course of the particular negotiation. Since there are no universal rules for negotiating, the applicable rules become whatever the parties agree on. They should address such issues as the confidentiality of the proceedings and the length, frequency, and location of the sessions.

Negotiations on the agenda and other process matters can color the whole course of the subsequent negotiations. Early agreement on these items may establish commitment to the process and momentum toward settlement. Conversely, a team can use this phase to manage the other side's expectations (*see infra* pp. 38-40). For example, it can conduct itself so as to make the other side think, "If they were that difficult in agreeing on an agenda, this will be one long and frustrating negotiation, and we're unlikely to get what we want out of it." Refusal to agree on the shape of the table at the Vietnamese peace talks in Geneva was meant to convey this message.

Of course, in the Case of the Unmanaged Negotiation, the teams did not conduct this joint preparation. If the EPA team had had even the most rudimentary advance discussions with TS, it might have avoided some of its mistakes. It need not have been embarrassed by having TS wait in the wrong place for half an hour. Nor would it have been boxed into a tight corner of a small room from which it was unable to caucus.

Managing Behavior

In preparing for a negotiation, the team leader's first task is to identify all the people who must be managed. (*See supra* pp. 6-7.) It is a nasty surprise to find that a forgotten and therefore unmanaged participant is a fly in the ointment when a settlement is almost within grasp. The main groups the team leader must manage are his or her own team (both members at the table and supporting members, such as experts); the client (including its relevant chain or chains of command); and outside groups that may have interests in or influence on the outcome of the negotiation (federal and state agencies, elected officials, public interest groups, corporations, trade associations, media). And, of course, the whole point of the exercise is to manage the other side.

Managing the Team

Team management is necessary both to get maximum benefit from team members and to assure that members don't inadvertently interfere with the team's effectiveness. As discussed *supra* p. 20, team management must start at the preparation stage. Before active negotiation with the other side begins, the team leader must:

- lead the team in developing negotiating objectives, strategies, and tactics;
- assure that all team members are thoroughly prepared on their aspects of the case;
- assure that all team members have shared their knowledge and experience; and
- lead the team in establishing basic rules by which it will govern itself during the negotiation.

The task of establishing basic team rules warrants special emphasis. There are few universal rules for team conduct, other than that team-specific rules are necessary and that members must agree to follow those rules. The team must establish two sets of ground rules:

- how to make decisions within the team, and
- how to handle communications outside the team.

Often the easiest rules for effective negotiation rest on the principles of internal decision by consensus and external communication by the team leader. As teams grow accustomed to and comfortable with functioning together, these rules may change. For example, team decisions need not be by consensus on matters all agree are unimportant, and different team members may be spokespersons on matters within their areas of expertise. However, it is critical that all team members present the same message to the outside world. (Even nonverbal communication must be consistent; the team leader's silver-tongued persuasion will be less than effective if the leader's own team members roll their eyes or yawn during it.) Two activities deserve special attention in this regard: caucusing and shadow bargaining.

☐ *Caucusing.* One rule of negotiation is close to absolute: The team must decide upon its course of action and resolve differences among its members internally, not in front of the other side. Nothing distinguishes unprepared, amateur negotiators from prepared professionals as much as discussion of internal team differences at the negotiating table. This kind of discussion gives the other team great advantages. Caucusing at the table can tell the other team who sides with it and who doesn't, who wants to settle and who doesn't, who is prepared and who isn't. The other team can then orient its tactics and presentation to support its friends on the disordered team. Indeed, it can participate directly in that team's discussions, as Larado did in the Case of the Unmanaged Negotiation. To avoid this kind of interference, teams should resolve their internal differences in private caucuses.

Caucusing is an important tool of team management. It can hardly be used enough. The authors have never seen it used too much. Caucuses aren't just used to avoid displaying dirty linen at the negotiating table. They can also be used:

- to share information in private;
- to regroup after a surprise;
- to let tempers cool;
- to get information or opinions from experts not at the table; and
- to clarify negotiating authority with the client.

Caucusing should be done away from the negotiating table and out of the negotiating room. Whispered corner conferences may feel private, but are they? Whispers often project to the other team, and body language usually does. A whispered "yes" or "no" with an accompanying head shake, for instance, is easy to discern at a distance. And you never know what interpretive skills the other side may have; the authors know one environmental lawyer who, for reasons completely unrelated to negotiation, has learned to read lips.

Team members must agree on how to signal for caucuses, and on how to call them without letting the other side know why. If you call a caucus just after the other side makes a major factual presentation, it may deduce that some of the facts it presented were new to you and require you to reassess your position. This knowledge could be of great strategic or tactical value to it. When the team leader wants to caucus or gets a caucus signal from a team member, the leader can change the subject under discussion and call a caucus a few minutes later. The purpose of the caucus then may not be evident to the other side. Alternatively, you can ask the other team to caucus to consider a presentation or proposal you have made. This gives you time to caucus, perhaps about a completely different issue. In an emergency, a spilled cup of coffee may break up the negotiation and enable a team to caucus without signaling the reason. Of course, there is a limit to how frequently you can use this tactic.

☐ *Shadow Bargaining.* Shadow bargaining is informal negotiating outside of official sessions, caucuses, and constituent meetings. (See Figure 5.) Sometimes shadow meetings are fully authorized by team members or key hierarchy members, and sometimes they are not. In one type of shadow bargaining, high-level team or hierarchy members meet privately to see whether they can make a deal. They may succeed in at least hammering out a general framework, because privacy

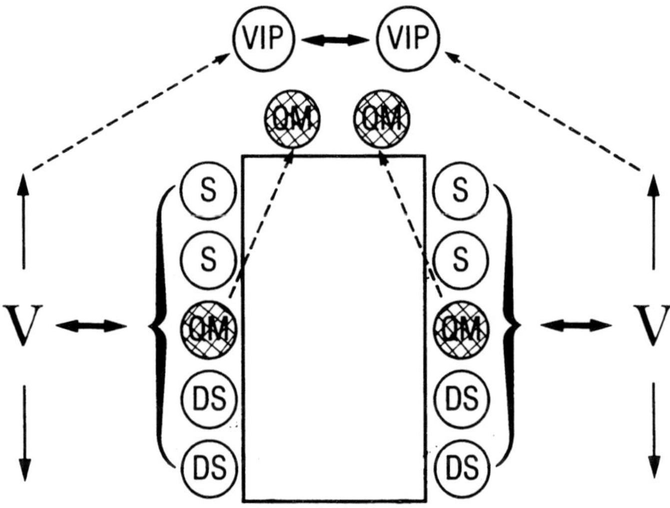

Figure 5: Shadow bargaining between team leaders (QMs) and between high-level client personnel (VIPs)

frees them from their "roles" of engaging in rhetoric or expounding on the virtues of their positions. However, unless known to and authorized by the team, such shadow meetings can be dangerous. Constituents, fearing a "sell-out," may reject any deal made. The shadow negotiators then lose considerable credibility with both sides; this in turn creates additional barriers to settlement.

Similarly, well-intentioned team or lower-level hierarchy members sometimes take it upon themselves to meet in an effort to facilitate agreement. Unless these individuals' mandates are clear and their authority agreed upon in advance, such meetings are more likely to yield misunderstandings and bad feelings than viable, workable agreements. Meetings of this type should therefore be avoided.

An activity closely related to shadow bargaining is the use of private communication channels. In many bargaining relationships, numerous such channels are available. These can often be very valuable if an impasse develops, but can pose problems if an unmanaged participant uses them to send the other side a false or misleading message.

The team leader must manage the team and the client hierarchy to avoid the problems associated with shadow bargaining and private communication channels. All such activities should be coordinated through the leader and carefully designed to advance team objectives.

Managing the Client's Hierarchy

Some of the toughest problems that negotiators face involve their own clients' organizations. All too often a client's chain of command consists of untrained, inexperienced negotiators who are unwilling to give the negotiation the time and attention it needs. This can make it impossible for the negotiating team to perform optimally. Although the team may not be able to overcome the problem, it often can do so with sufficient effort, and it usually can at least improve the situation.

Management of the client's hierarchy begins at the preparation stage. Initially the team leader must identify what chain of command is involved and how much of it is likely to or must become involved in the case in any real sense. This step can be difficult if the client has multiple hierarchies or has members with potentially competing interests. As an example of the multiple-hierarchy problem, consider a hazardous waste case involving surface water contamination and issues of statutory interpretation. For the government to settle such a case, concurrence may be required from both regional and headquarters personnel for the RCRA program office, the CERCLA program office, the Water program office, Enforcement, General Counsel, and the Department of Justice. Some cases will also involve the Administrator.

Even if a negotiating team leader accurately identifies all the members of such an unwieldy and potentially conflicting set of hierarchies, few team leaders will have the organizational stature to orchestrate them all. But the leader can and must identify the parts of the organizational structure that should be involved in a case and are necessary to its resolution. The leader can then work with his or her own superiors to get other hierarchies productively involved.

The client's hierarchy must be managed so that it will:

- assign the appropriate team members;
- provide the necessary resources;
- agree in advance on settlement objectives;
- be flexible regarding settlement objectives as circumstances change;
- engage in shadow bargaining only under the strict control of the team leader;
- prevent end runs to the top of the organization, or at least blunt their potential disruption; and
- approve a settlement recommended by the team.

Under some circumstances the team will also need the chain of command to do other things, such as modify an existing policy to accommodate a specific situation. The better the team manages the client's hierarchy, the likelier the hierarchy is to provide support and agreement when needed.

The team manages the client's hierarchy by:

- communicating with it;

- keeping it informed of developments; and
- gaining its advance concurrence in positions taken.

Under some circumstances, the team will employ additional techniques similar to those that it uses in negotiating with its opposition.

A team frequently devotes more time and effort to negotiating with its client's hierarchy than to negotiating with the other side. Although this can sometimes be discouraging, remember that it is one of a negotiator's basic tasks, and that the other team is probably facing very similar difficulties.

Managing Other Players

There are two other types of players that must be managed: those at the table, and those not at the table.

☐ *Negotiators at the Table.* Many environmental negotiations involve multiple parties. Frequently, some of those parties have mutual interests. For example, when EPA and a state environmental agency are involved in a negotiation, they normally act as partners. Similarly, a subgroup of PRPs may cooperate among themselves. In such a situation, the allied parties may be viewed together and managed as one loose negotiating team. Although this is obviously more difficult than managing an effort that is all under one roof, it is doubly necessary to assure that the other side does not divide and conquer the potential allies.

To manage their effort most effectively, the allies must first identify their common ground and any differences they may have. They should then develop negotiating objectives that are mutually supportive rather than destructive. Finally, they should determine how best to organize themselves and who should take the lead overall or on particular issues.

A multilateral bargaining model (based on the simple bilateral bargaining model discussed *supra* pp. 6-7) may help the negotiator understand and manage multi-party negotiations. Each party to such a negotiation conducts its own horizontal, internal, and vertical bargaining. Each increase in the number of parties thus geometrically increases the total number of bargaining configurations and the complexity of the negotiation process.

Each increase also creates new possibilities for strategic alliances. For example, in a trilateral (three-sided) negotiation, two sides may reach an agreement that threatens the interests of the third. (See Figure 6.) In a quadrilateral (four-sided) negotiation, more configurations

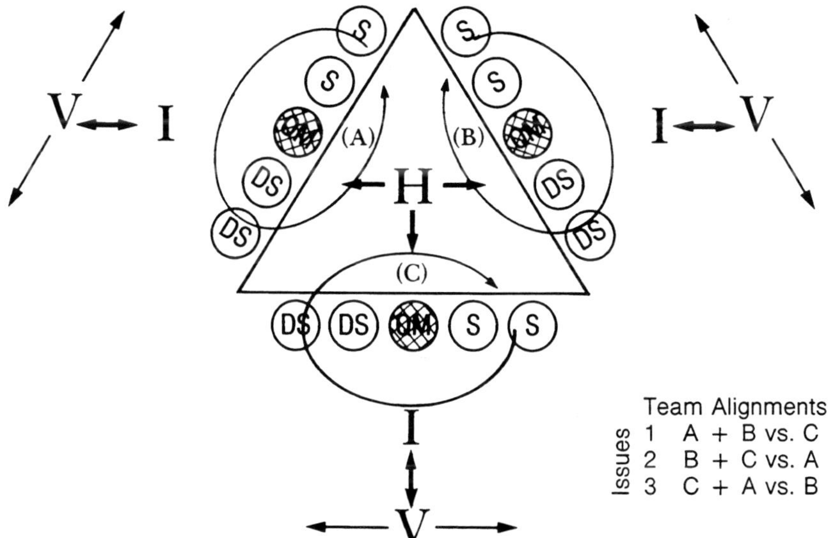

Figure 6: Trilateral bargaining

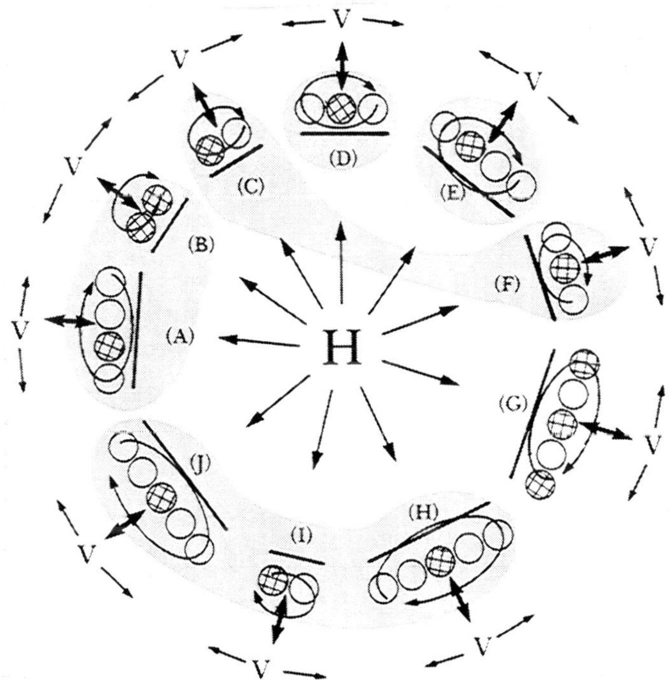

Figure 7: Multilateral bargaining (showing potential team alignments)

are possible, including various permutations of two against two and three against one. Of course, negotiations aren't limited to four parties; there may be forty or four hundred. Negotiations among numerous parties are sometimes called "hydralateral" negotiations, after the mythological monster that grew two heads to replace any one that was cut off. Complex environmental negotiations often fit this description. (See Figure 7.)

In multilateral negotiations, alignments and alliances may shift from issue to issue. Although coalitions may form on individual issues, the ultimate goal is full consensus among all parties on all issues. In this regard, the possibility of some parties coalescing against others may look like the major weakness of the multilateral process, but may actually be its major strength. As each party seeks to build bridges and achieve coalitions to control vital issues, it becomes more sensitive to the other parties' needs. This sensitivity in turn facilitates multiparty consensus.

An increase in the number of parties also makes shadow bargaining more problematic. Each party must continually question whether it should meet informally with just one or some of the other parties, or with all of them; whether it should meet with the other parties separately or together; whether it should inform each party of a meeting with another; and, if so, how much of the discussion it should share. Moreover, an increase in the number of players increases the chances that unauthorized individuals will meet and make commitments or seek consensus on their own. When multiple parties are involved, the trust and good faith so critical to the exchange of promises are especially fragile, unstable, difficult to achieve, and easily threatened by shadow bargaining.

□ *Negotiators Not at the Table.* There may be "phantom" players in a negotiation, players who are not directly represented at the table or in the client's hierarchy, but who are nonetheless interested in the negotiation and able to influence it. The more significant or controversial the case, the more numerous the phantom players are likely to be. They are particularly common in environmental cases. In citizen suits, for instance, EPA and the state agency may be phantom players. In government enforcement actions, phantom players may include legislators, staff from the White House or governor's mansion, other federal or state departments or agencies, special interest groups, and the media.

Phantom players can pose several problems. For one thing, the negotiation process works best and most efficiently in private. Privacy makes it easier to avoid grandstanding, to build trust, to be flexible, to take risks, and to compromise. The greater the role of phantom players, the likelier the negotiations are to be conducted in a fishbowl. While official players are constrained to treat negotiations as confidential, phantom players are not. Indeed, publicizing information on the progress of negotiations often serves these players' interests, which may range from getting publicity for its own sake to embarrassing a party into changing its position or even to preventing a settlement. Proper management by a negotiating team may minimize, but cannot always eliminate, unconstructive public disclosures by a phantom. (*See infra* p. 42.)

In order to deal most effectively with phantom players, a negotiating team should determine early who they are likely to be and how much they may influence the negotiation process. The team's primary task regarding these players is to make sure they know they are not parties to the negotiation and will not be treated as such. They may be able to give the team valuable information, however. If appropriate, the team can listen to their views. In some cases, it can assure them that those views will be carefully considered. Occasionally, it should assure them that they will be briefed on the outcome and told how their views were considered and addressed. But they seldom should be advised of the course of the negotiation as it develops or be consulted as decisions are made. Few phantom players—even interested senators and members of Congress—really expect this, but they will take it and more if they can get it. The negotiating team must know when and how to say "no," and must manage the client's hierarchy so that it will affirm a "no."

Apart from these general tactics, each phantom player must be dealt with individually. Different types of players have different levels of interest in, and influence over, negotiation outcomes. Elected officials, for example, usually seek audiences with regulators on behalf of constituents only to show the constituents that they have the power to gain access and are willing to use it for their benefit. These officials rarely want to become involved in the merits of enforcement disputes. Even when they do, they usually do not have great leverage. Sometimes, however, they may be determined to see that a particular resolution is reached, and sometimes they do have leverage.

In contrast, public interest groups or concerned local citizens often are not content with gaining access or airing their views. Their concerns may go far beyond the particular dispute under negotiation. They may be forces to be reckoned with if they have undeniably meritorious positions or proven access to court or the political process. In some instances, their opposition may make a settlement difficult to consummate or more trouble than it is worth.

Managing Time: The Importance of Deadlines

There is an old lawyer's saying that "90 percent of cases settle on the courthouse steps." It might be more accurate to say that 90 percent of negotiations settle in the last 10 percent of the time allowed for them. Both sayings make two points about timing in negotiations:

- unmanaged negotiations tend to drag on forever, and
- deadlines energize the negotiation process.

Effective management of negotiations must include establishment and enforcement of deadlines.

Most people assigned to negotiate environmental disputes have many other assignments and cannot be expected to devote full time to any one negotiation. Because this is usually true of all the members of each team, there is often no one meeting time really convenient for everyone. It is no wonder that negotiations left to their own devices tend to drag on forever, taking months to resolve what could be handled in a few weeks of concerted effort. Deferral of resolution is usually not attributable to bad faith or conscious foot-dragging (although delay often does benefit one side more than another, as when it allows a defendant to postpone expenditures). However, loss of momentum may make the side that should be dominant settle on easier terms just to resolve the case. And options may close as time passes and each side proceeds along its own course. Options among remedies narrow, for instance, as a defendant begins to implement a particular remedy. Penalty cases become less compelling as they grow stale or compliance is achieved.

The normal way to expedite resolution of negotiations is to establish and adhere to deadlines. The ultimate deadline is the commencement of a trial or the rendering of a verdict. Good time management will usually aim to avoid this deadline and resolve disputes much earlier, before resources are diverted to discovery and trial preparation. Deadlines should be set for specific actions, including ultimate resolution of the dispute as well as interim milestones along the way. They should allow reasonable periods for these actions, but their violation should carry specific penalties. The government can easily set deadlines in enforcement cases because it controls the timing of enforcement activities: issuance of orders, filing of complaints, deposition of companies' officers, etc. Private parties involved in negotiations should also establish deadlines. They have fewer enforcement options than the government does, but they are not helpless. Any action that the other party wants to avoid, such as the issuance of an unfavorable press release or the filing of an unwanted motion in court, can serve as an effective sanction for violating a deadline. Deadlines and their sanctions are, of course, themselves subject to negotiation.

Management of milestones during a protracted negotiation may require considerable judgment. For example, a threat to file a complaint if settlement is not reached by a date certain should not be slavishly carried out if settlement is close, good progress is being made, and the other side is not dragging its feet. Under these circumstances, filing the complaint will discourage the other side and may slacken the pace of the negotiation, because the other side will no longer have an inducement for quick action and both sides will have to divert attention to litigation. Once a threat is carried out, it loses all its power to force action. At the same time, if deadlines routinely pass with no follow-through on threatened sanctions, they will soon lose their credibility and usefulness.

Finally, you may on occasion wish to extend a deadline yourself. You can do this either by negotiating a new deadline or by pursuing any of a number of delaying tactics. Asking a court for a restraining order, for example, will usually slow the negotiation down. Remember, however, that if you take any delaying action that the other side perceives as unfair, you may lose your credibility and terminate the negotiation entirely.

Managing the Process or System

Management of the negotiation process is important. It can improve a team's position in a settlement. It can also improve negotiating efficiency, moving a dispute along to quick settlement with few diversions.

Recognizing and Projecting Power

It is a truism among negotiators that "the lion gets the lion's share and the lamb gets the lamb's share." Consider how much you negotiated with the bank when you got your last home mortgage. You'd have negotiated a lot more, however, if you had been a business negotiating a multi-million-dollar financing from the same bank.

Power is a critical asset in a negotiation. The side with the most power usually gets most of what it wants. Maximizing a client's power and using it to the full will produce a settlement satisfactory to the client. Squandering or failing to appreciate that power won't. Managing power begins with recognizing where it lies and figuring out how to use it.

When the government is a party to a dispute, it usually has most of the perceived power. It can decide whether, when, and on what terms to issue a permit, for example. If someone challenges its decision, courts will give it considerable deference. The government can also decide whether to impose or seek a sanction and, if so, what type of sanction—a small penalty, a severe penalty, or jail time. And in a dispute that it doesn't want to lose, the government can mobilize almost boundless resources.

This array of government power can be formidable, but it is not insurmountable. This is true for several reasons. Most importantly, power is a perception, not a corporeal reality. If a negotiating party, even a government party, isn't perceived as having power, it doesn't have it for purposes of that negotiation. In a compliance dispute, for example, the regulated party may not believe the government will use an available sanction, either because the government has not established a credible enforcement record or because its negotiators don't project a credible threat. In either case the government's negotiating team will lose the power it should have had.

Some government negotiators are uncomfortable with asserting their client's full power. This discomfort is often expressed in statements such as, "We really would like a penalty of around $X." This, of course, is just what Laura said in the Case of the Unmanaged Negotiation. While it may sound polite to the speaker, it sends a mixed signal to the listener. It is not a demand. It doesn't sound as serious as a demand. It must mean the speaker really isn't serious. Unexpected politeness in this context too often will be perceived as weakness. For example, Larado clearly saw Laura's statement as an admission of weakness and an invitation to drive for a much lower penalty. (*See infra* pp. 38-40.)

Furthermore, although private parties may be perceived to have little power in comparison to the government, they can enhance their power in many ways. Preparation, knowledge of facts and law, and negotiating skills can all confer power, as can management of the negotiation process. Sometimes the nature of one party's interests gives the other party power. For example, if the government is critically interested in having a private defendant pay for a quick cleanup, the defendant may have power to obtain other concessions in exchange for doing so. Knowledge of and willingness to resort to alternatives to negotiation can also confer power. For example, public interest groups have little power in any formal sense. They aren't invested with authority and have little economic clout. But they gain power in negotiations by their well-known willingness to pursue their issues single-mindedly through lobbying and litigation. Again, the secret of exerting power in a negotiation is credibility. Since power is perceptual, you have it if, and only if, you credibly convey that you have it and will use it. The real power in any negotiation is the negotiator's ability to be believed.

Projecting and using power doesn't mean being overbearing or inflexible. An overbearing attitude borders on arrogance—it isn't attractive, and it breeds resentment and contempt. Inflexibility needlessly inhibits creative and mutually satisfactory settlements. Instead, projecting power simply requires self-confident awareness of the client's interests and its right and ability to secure or protect those interests.

Managing Significant Functions

Managing the negotiation process requires recognizing management functions and seizing the initiative to perform or assign them. Many of these functions have been discussed already. They include:

- establishing a goal, a strategy, objectives, and tactics;
- drafting an agenda;
- establishing ground rules for the negotiation;
- making initial contact with the other side;
- arranging the logistics of the first negotiating session;
- making introductions and the opening statement at the first session;
- appointing a team member as timekeeper and another as recorder;
- establishing a schedule and deadlines for the negotiation; and
- drafting the settlement papers.

☐ *Selecting the Meeting Place.* Is the meeting place important? It was in the Case of the Unmanaged Negotiation. The room was too small to house the negotiators comfortably. The EPA negotiators were cut off from the door and could not easily leave the room to caucus.

Two sets of considerations influence the selection of a meeting room: those that benefit both sides, and those that primarily benefit the side managing the selection. The first set applies in all negotiations, but is particularly important in protracted negotiations. The room should be comfortable and conducive to good communications and hard work. It should not have diversions such as excessive noise, foot traffic, or scenery. It should be close to a caucusing area with telephones. If paperwork is to be done at the meeting, it should be close to the necessary logistical support, including after-hours support if sessions are expected to last into the evening.

The second set of considerations is more complex. Assuming that appropriate rooms are available at several locations, choice of location can send any of a number of messages. Negotiating in the client's offices, for example, emphasizes the client's power. A government party can enhance this effect by meeting at the office of the U.S. Attorney or the Attorney General. Negotiating at the site of a problem may facilitate understanding and resolution. Meeting on the other side's territory may make it more comfortable and easier to deal with. Alternating meetings between the two teams' territories lends an aura of fairness and even-handedness. Meeting on "neutral ground" such as a hotel conference room conveys a similar message, and can help reduce tensions in a difficult negotiation.

□ *Arranging the Players.* Do room arrangements contribute to negotiating dynamics? Very definitely. While there is no hard and fast rule on what table shape or seating configuration is best, different arrangements will facilitate different dynamics. The meeting host should therefore plan these arrangements in advance. For example, if there are more than two teams, the host can help "divide and conquer" natural allies by separating them physically, or can help them act together by seating them together.

Putting teams on opposite sides of a room puts distance between them, causes hearing difficulties unless voices are raised, and is not conducive to building good working relationships between the teams. Using a round table makes the atmosphere less adversarial and facilitates working relationships. Other configurations create their own dynamics. For example, in some experiments conducted by the American Arbitration Association, negotiations seemed to go more smoothly when parties sat in comfortable chairs with no or very low tables between them.

Any arrangement, of course, is subject to negotiation when the meeting begins. The team that silently acquiesces to sitting in low chairs with the sun in its eyes is apt to have a more than physically uncomfortable negotiation.

□ *Controlling the Negotiating Record.* A team can gain power by its use of its designated note-taker. If the team leader occasionally calls on the note-taker to read back exactly what was said at some juncture, the note-taker becomes the unofficial historian of the sessions (unless challenged). This can be a critical source of power when questions arise on past agreements. This tactic is effective only if the note-taker's notes are made perfect by the entire team during their caucus after each session. The note-taker can also enhance the team's power in other ways. For example, the team leader can defuse outbursts—or even slow the momentum, and thus blunt the effectiveness, of presentations—by asking the other side to slow down or repeat its words so the note-taker can keep up. Another way to control the negotiating record is to summarize the discussion at the end of each session, and to ask whether there are any items not included in your summary. This makes it harder for the other side to put new issues on the table at the eleventh hour.

☐ *Drafting the Settlement Papers.* Drafting settlement papers is often an important method of exerting control and improving bargaining position. If you draft the papers, the other side bears the burden of challenging your presentation and of raising, arguing for, and justifying every change, no matter how small. Sometimes, however, there may be reasons to let the other side draft the papers. If the relationship is already sensitive, insistence on drafting the papers yourself may damage it further, making agreement more difficult. The other side may also gain a false sense of confidence from being the initial drafter. The other side may have a superlative drafter who is demonstrably fair and can hasten the process along. The other side may have a more thorough grasp of certain important facts, in which case it may save time to have that side draft the sections involving those facts.

Effective Bargaining

Parties who bargain effectively may achieve better results from negotiation than from litigation. In any dispute, some issues may be subject to objective standards, but others will be open to a wider range of resolutions. For example, there can't be much bargaining about meeting a regulatory standard, unless its application is unclear. But the means of, and schedule for, achieving the standard may be open to bargaining, as are the amount of any penalty and the terms of any agreement that either party desires and the law does not require. By bargaining effectively, a party may both optimize its positions regarding legal requirements and secure benefits beyond those expressly authorized by law. A government agency, in particular, can often use its leverage and power effectively to negotiate for sanctions or concessions beyond those authorized by the statute it is enforcing. In the Case of the Unmanaged Negotiation, for example, Laura and Sam had considerable leverage based on TS's need for a clean environmental record to get financing for its incinerators. If they had known about this leverage, they could have used it to get a substantial penalty or perhaps a concession outside the bounds of the statute, such as posting of a performance bond or performance of research on new compliance methods.

☐ *Creating and Managing Doubts and Uncertainties.* The successful negotiator is one who effectively makes others doubt the viability of their own positions. Indeed, doubt creation can be viewed as the negotiator's chief job. Only if they doubt their own positions will the negotiator's team members, client hierarchy, and opponents see any need to consider the negotiator's position or make any movement toward it.

Like every other key aspect of the negotiation process, doubt creation must be managed. The negotiator doesn't want others to have so many doubts that they simply retreat in disarray, afraid to agree to any settlement. And, of course, the negotiator doesn't want others to doubt the viability of his or her own position. Thus, doubt creation must not be indiscriminate. Many of the suggestions in this monograph can be read as ways to create and manage doubts.

☐ *Managing Expectations.* By explaining in Chapter One that there are limits on learning negotiation from books, we hopefully managed your expectations of what you would learn from this monograph. If you had expected the monograph to make you an instant negotiation star, you would have been disappointed with it. But if we succeeded in lowering your expectations, you will be satisfied with it. The monograph hasn't changed; only your expectations have.

Successful negotiation requires similar management of expectations. In a normal negotiation, each side begins with expectations about the other side's demands. If you do nothing to manage what the other team expects to get from you, it may expect a lot and be unwilling to settle for a little. But if you manage its expectations before even sitting down at the negotiating table, it may find a little quite satisfactory. Before you can manage all parties' expectations, of course, you must be patient and take the time to learn what they are.

The importance of managing expectations becomes clear when the consequences of mismanaging them are understood. The discussion below focuses on these consequences in the context of negotiations over penalties. Of course, penalties are not the only issue on which expectations should be managed. Similar techniques, appropriately tailored to the particular negotiation at hand, may be used to manage expectations on other issues. And private parties may use tactics similar to those recommended below for the government.

Inexperienced government negotiators sometimes appear reluctant to initiate discussions of penalties, to demand high penalties, or to refer to penalty demands at the outset of negotiations, as if there were something unseemly about penalties or only "headquarters" cared about them. This reluctance creates an expectation that penalties are not seriously sought or that insignificant amounts will be accepted, particularly if the parties reach agreement on all other issues. Later insistence on significant penalties will catch the other side completely unprepared. Indeed, its negotiating team will probably have told its client's hierarchy that penalties aren't a big issue. Forcing the team to reverse itself now will demolish its credibility with that hierarchy.

This type of problem has arisen frequently in practice negotiations observed by the authors, primarily because inexperienced negotiators sent mixed signals to their opponents. (*See supra* p. 34.) For example, when one "government" team decided it needed a $50,000 penalty, its lead negotiator said to the other side, in an almost apologetic voice, "We really would like to get a penalty of around $50,000." The other side took this to mean that the government team wasn't serious about stiff penalties and didn't expect to get anything close to $50,000. It assumed that agreement could easily be reached in the $10,000 to $15,000 range, its own limit, and went on to iron out technical matters. When penalties were finally discussed again at the end of the session, it was shocked to find the government team unyielding at $50,000. It thought the government team had misled it. One member thought the government spokesperson had acted in bad faith. No settlement was reached by the end of the session. In fact, some of the technical agreements reached earlier had begun to unravel.

In an enforcement matter, the government team should make clear at the outset of the first negotiating session that it expects a penalty, and should specify the range of acceptable amounts. The defendant will usually expect the government's initial penalty demand to be at least twice as much as the government is actually willing to settle for. Therefore, the government should normally start with a demand at least twice as high as the minimum that it is willing to accept, and should be adamant about it from the beginning. The defendant's team will hope it can cut that amount in half, but because of the government's insistent demands and justifications, it won't be sure. Instead, it will prepare its client for the bitter pill of paying close to what the government asks. As the government eventually lets the defendant whittle away at the penalty amount, the defendant's team will be pleased with its progress, will appear to its client to be doing a good job, and may readily agree to a penalty higher than the government's goal.

This strategy requires the government to be firm, but not necessarily harsh. In order to appear flexible and create a better atmosphere for negotiation, the government may frame its initial penalty demand in terms of a general description—e.g., "high six figures"— and a characterization of the reasons justifying this amount—e.g., "long-standing, deliberate, calculated refusal to comply"; "good faith efforts to overcome technological difficulties"; "significant health hazard." Even if the government uses this gentler approach, however, it must state its penalty demand clearly at the beginning of the negotiation, not camouflage it until the end.

By the same token, the defendant's negotiating team should manage the government's expectations on penalties. The government won't expect an initial offer anywhere close to either its initial demand or the defendant's bottom line. If the government demands $50,000 and the defendant immediately offers $30,000, the government will expect to settle for $40,000. It will perceive that the defendant believes its demand is not unreasonably off the mark for the violation alleged and that the defendant is willing to pay more than $30,000. If the defendant refuses to pay more than $30,000, the negotiation will probably fail. On the other hand, if the defendant makes no initial offer but counters with a series of credible assertions or facts (e.g., it has never voluntarily paid a penalty to any governmental entity and has resolved at the highest level never to do so, or a respected court has just awarded a $5000 penalty for a similar violation), it will lower the government's expectations considerably. The government may ultimately be happy with a $20,000 settlement.

The other side's expectations can be managed not only by the negotiators, but by the client's general policies and public pronouncements. For instance, EPA's penalty policy is a significant effort to manage expectations in terms of both the general framework for setting penalties and the amounts EPA expects to recover. While the policy has not created the expectation that EPA will actually recover the economic benefit of delayed compliance when that benefit is measured in the millions of dollars, it has created the expectation that EPA will seek and secure significantly higher penalties than it has in the past. EPA negotiators may capitalize on this general expectation to manage expectations in an individual negotiation. For instance, in advance of the first negotiating session, they can send a copy of the policy to the other side and request it to furnish the figures needed to calculate the benefit of delayed compliance.

Note, however, that techniques for managing expectations must be tailored to particular situations. For example, while sending the other side a copy of a relevant policy may help lower expectations in one case, it may raise them in another by alerting the recipient to loopholes in the policy. Similarly, sending the other side a statement of your company's financial condition may help lower the other side's expectations in one case, but may raise them in another if this condition is better than it had anticipated.

☐ *Managing Concessions.* A negotiating team can also strengthen its bargaining position by carefully managing the concessions it makes. To do this, the team must first inventory the concessions it *can* make. Be creative in compiling this inventory. You may even be able to invent concessions that don't exist. For example, the government can say, "We will agree not to commence contractor debarment proceedings if you do X," when it really had no intention of initiating such proceedings. A private party can similarly offer to forbear from filing a motion or claim that it had no intention of actually filing.

After inventorying its potential concessions, the team must decide when and how to make them. In general, a team should only make a concession if it gains something in return. The trade doesn't necessarily have to be "even"— indeed, concessions are often difficult to value, and are worth different amounts to the giver and the receiver. A negotiator can often enhance the value of a concession by withholding it. Therefore, if the other team seeks a concession of no great value to you, don't automatically give it away; you may not know how much it is worth to them. The harder and longer they press for it, the more value it assumes in their minds. At some point they may be willing to make a concession valuable to you in return for it. Conversely, if the other team withholds a concession you want, bear in mind that they may be trying to get you to pay more for it than it is really worth to you. If you recognize this technique, you can avoid falling victim to it.

Of course, effective management may sometimes involve making seemingly gratuitous concessions. Such concessions are often made toward the beginning of the bargaining phase. They may establish good will and signal the team's willingness to bargain or be flexible. Even these concessions, however, must be considered and managed. Is a particular concession likely to achieve the desired result? Is it the smallest concession necessary to achieve that result? Is the result worth the concession?

When approaching a concession, compromise, or bargain, don't commit yourself until you're sure you are getting exactly what you want out of it. The use of questions rather than statements can help avoid premature commitments. For example, the question, "If I do X, will you do Y?" is as effective in exploring a possible trade as the statement, "I'll do X if you'll do Y," and is much less committal. In addition, you should usually let the other side propose the final settlement. This puts you in the catbird seat of accepting or rejecting their proposal. You should accept it only after you paraphrase it carefully to make sure it is what you want.

Managing Public Pronouncements

Like communications to the other side, communications to the media can be either useful or harmful. It is therefore important to manage the public pronouncements made by your client's hierarchy and by other players.

There should be only one public spokesperson for each side in a negotiation, and all inquiries should be routed to that person. Often the best spokesperson is the team leader, and the next best someone in the client's press office who has been trained in the sensitivity of matters under negotiation.

The team and its client must also reach agreement on what can and cannot be said. Often they must take care not to give the other side information publicly that it has not been able to get in the negotiation. One of the authors recalls leaving a negotiating session wondering what concession his client would have to make to obtain a compliance schedule extension that the EPA team had adamantly refused. The next day, before returning to the negotiation to offer an appropriate concession, the author read in the newspaper a statement by an unnamed EPA official that the existing schedule was infeasible and would be extended.

There are other pitfalls to avoid as well. Chief among them is grandstanding. If you paint yourself into a corner by publicly promising a certain result at the outset of negotiations, it will be harder for you to adjust your position based on what you learn during them.

Unfortunately, managing public pronouncements can be difficult. Some in your organization or in your client's hierarchy may be overly fond of being quoted in the press, and many reporters are skilled at getting more information than an interviewee intended to give. Public statements by phantom players are even harder to control than statements by your own client. (*See supra* pp. 30-31.) In some cases, it is wise to cut off communications with a loose-tongued phantom. In others, keeping communications open may leave you in a better position to manage the phantom's future public statements.

Chapter 5: Effective Communication

Aside from credibility, what is the negotiator's most important tool? Communication. Through communication, primarily verbal communication, you can manage expectations, create doubts, educate, persuade, trade proposals, and reach agreement. To bring the other side around to your point of view, you have to talk, and talk effectively and believably.

Non-verbal communication is also important. Inflection and body language can verify, supplement, or contradict spoken words. We've all seen people say "yes" with their lips but "no" with their eyes. We usually believe the eyes. On another level, a grim-faced, steely-eyed, clenched-jawed pose may effectively express disinterest in negotiation, hostility toward the other side, or rejection of a proposal. But it may not help change the other side's point of view.

Negotiating Styles and Attitudes

Is there a perfect negotiating style? Or one that is best for government officials? For regulated entities? For public interest groups? As with so many other aspects of negotiation, hard and fast rules are rare.

There are as many negotiating styles as there are personalities. Nevertheless, a composite of key elements from most styles can be plotted on a spectrum from cooperative to aggressive. At one end is the wimp who concedes every point. At the other is the obnoxious gunslinger whom no one trusts or likes. Most of us are somewhere in between.

Professor Gerald Williams of Brigham Young University conducted a study in Phoenix of the effectiveness of attorneys' negotiating styles.[1] Attorneys were asked to rank the degree of success achieved

1. G. Williams, Legal Negotiation and Settlement (1983).

by the attorneys opposing them in their latest negotiations. They also rated their opponents on over a hundred characteristics that enabled the researchers to locate their styles on the cooperative-aggressive spectrum. Sixty-five percent of the negotiators were rated as cooperative, and fifty percent of those were ranked as effective by their opponents. Twenty-five percent were rated as aggressive, and only twenty-five percent of those were ranked as effective. Thus, while cooperativeness does not guarantee success, it may make it easier. At the same time, while the aggressive attorneys succeeded less often, their successes were often greater than those achieved by their cooperative colleagues.

Since many different negotiating styles can be successful, it is probably most effective to be yourself when negotiating, maximizing and capitalizing on your own strengths. Remember, a successful negotiation requires trust, and it's easier to trust people who are being themselves. Some, the born "hams" among us, may naturally take on different styles in different situations. A cooperative approach may be more effective when difficult technical issues must be understood and evaluated. A more aggressive approach may produce better penalty results in enforcement negotiations. Changing styles during the course of a negotiation can also be effective. When the mild-mannered, polite, rational negotiator suddenly reaches the end of his tether and explodes, people tend to take him seriously.

Regardless of whether you use a cooperative or an aggressive style, you must establish credibility. The Brigham Young study found that honest and trustworthy behavior was a primary characteristic of successful negotiators of all styles.

Effective Listening

Why should a negotiator worry about listening? Because negotiation is conducted by oral communication, and oral communication requires listening as well as speaking. Two sides speaking at the same time do not communicate. In a negotiation, "a person's word is their bond," and you need to hear that word. Japanese negotiating teams, for example, are so conscious of the importance of listening that they generally do not respond to presentations or arguments before caucusing. Because they are not trying to plan their responses while the other side is talking, they can focus completely on listening to and evaluating what the other side is saying.

The effective listener enjoys several negotiating advantages. First, he or she takes in not only what is said but what isn't, including inflections, body language, messages between the lines, unstated assumptions, perceptions, misperceptions, and missing facts. Effective listening captures not only the words spoken, but the thinking behind them. It enables the listener to determine the weak points and blind spots in the other side's case, the points where doubts may most easily be created.

Moreover, just by listening attentively and with empathy, the effective listener encourages others to talk. The more the other side talks, the more you learn about it and its case. Let's face it—you already know what *you* know. It's smart to use negotiation as a "discovery process" to learn what the other side knows.

There are many techniques for improving team and individual listening skills.

- Ask only questions that can't be answered with a "yes" or "no." Longer answers almost always tell you more.
- Show empathy for the other side. Empathy prompts people to talk more.
- Paraphrase what the other side says. If you don't understand it the way they do, they will say so.
- Summarize at the end of the session and ask if there are any items not included in your summary. Like paraphrasing, summarizing surfaces different perceptions, avoids unnecessary misunderstandings, and makes it harder for the other team to change its mind later.
- Appoint a listener/note-taker whose only job is to observe. The very activity of taking notes enhances listening effectiveness. Over time the listener will observe more about the other side than will anyone else on your team. The listener will pick up the nuances of the other team's presentation, and will know from the glazed or attentive looks in its eyes which of your arguments or approaches it discounts or treats seriously. During caucus, the observer can help redirect the team's efforts toward the most productive tactics. The observer also helps maintain his or her own team's discipline. He or she can see, for example, when the body language of team members undercuts what the team spokesperson is saying. (Note-takers also have other uses; *see supra* pp. 19, 36-37.)

Effective Persuasion

On issue after issue, you must make the other side doubt the viability of its position and recognize the viability of yours. You can do this by arguing, questioning, and presenting facts. Inexperienced negotiators often don't understand these options and relapse into making speeches, stating positions, and repeating bold assertions. This is acceptable and normal at the beginning of the first negotiating session, when each team leader gives a speech building a persuasive case for the moral rectitude of his or her team's position. However, the speech is primarily for the home team's consumption; it is frequently not a serious attempt to influence the other side. After the opening speeches, negotiators must turn to subtler persuasive tools.

Argument and Questioning

We are all familiar with argument, and attorneys are well-schooled in it. Argument has its place in negotiation, but it is frequently counterproductive. Argument without sound factual underpinnings is usually self-defeating. Even good argument, supported by facts, often is not as effective as questioning. By arguing, you are trying to cause the other side to doubt its position on an issue: "You can't tell me it costs $25,000 to install a monitoring well. It only costs $10,000. That's what it cost at the X42 plant next door." But this argument is coming from you, the opposition, and for that reason alone it may be rejected and provoke a counterargument. You can make the point more effectively through questions: "Would it cost much more to install monitoring wells here than at the X42 plant next door?" Probably not. "Do you know what it cost there?" No. "I think it only cost $10,000. Why not call its plant manager and check?" Using questions develops your argument in the minds of the other side's team members, just where you want the thoughts (or doubts) to grow. It's the Socratic technique familiar to all students—a powerful educational device when divorced from the ego-deflating putdowns too often employed by prima donna professors. Of course, just as in a trial, you should be careful about asking questions if you do not know what the answers will be and where they will lead. You must remain in control of your questioning.

Knowing how powerful the questioning technique can be, you should be alert to the other team's use of it. Be aware that a seemingly innocent question may be designed to lead you into accepting an argument that will damage your side, and be very careful in framing your answers.

Facts and "Facts"

Facts are crucial in most environmental disputes. Facts determine what regulations apply, and how. They also determine other critical issues, such as whether a site should become a Superfund site and how it should be remedied. Effective factual presentations can therefore be of great value, especially in complicated matters. Because facts can play such important persuasive roles, their presentation should be carefully orchestrated. Pictures, charts, maps, graphs, and schematics help clarify the meaning of factual data—or the meaning consistent with your position. Such aids are essential if the alternative is an incoherent morass of data.

A litigator will often want to withhold a fact from the other side in a negotiation if the fact may be useful in litigation. If this issue arises, the team needs to examine its priorities. If settlement is the priority and the fact could help secure a settlement, it should ordinarily be used in the negotiation. If the dispute is later litigated, the fact will usually come out in formal discovery anyway.

In negotiating sessions, information is often asserted without verification. Nonetheless, it is usually accepted as factual. Recognizing that unrebutted or unquestioned assertions may be treated as facts gives a negotiator a key advantage. The negotiator can often establish critical "facts" merely by making and repeating assertions. This technique is not infallible—the other side may question the assertions—but it often succeeds. Of course, the negotiator should not make assertions that he or she cannot back up. If the negotiator is called on an assertion that is unverifiable or wrong, his or her credibility and trustworthiness will be greatly diminished not only in that negotiation, but in future negotiations for other clients. Remember, the real power in any negotiation is the power to be believed. Of course, the negotiator should also understand the importance of questioning the other side's assertions on critical issues before they become accepted "facts." In short, it is important to remember that "facts" are negotiable. So are "non-facts."

These points were illustrated in a recent negotiation by one of the authors on an air pollution enforcement matter. At a preparation session, the client anticipated that EPA would want it to operate with one rather than two machines to reduce emissions until it achieved final compliance. The client would lose money on one machine and simply shut down the whole operation. However, for a variety of unrelated but legitimate reasons, the client did not wish to lay out its economics before EPA at that time. The client was very worried about how to address the issue. The author told the client not to worry: the assertion that the operation was not viable on one machine would, when repeated, become an established fact. The client did not believe it. The assertion was made twice in the first negotiating session, was accepted, and thereafter was treated as a fact.

Chapter 6: Changing Policies, Changing Faces

Continuity is critically important in negotiations. Lack of continuity can make a negotiating team function less efficiently, impairing the team's performance and results. It can also destroy trust between teams, jeopardizing the possibility of achieving a settlement at all.

Breaks in continuity are common, however. The people and policies involved in negotiations change frequently. Other relevant factors, including statutes, regulations, and parties, can also change. Negotiators are responsible for preventing these changes from jeopardizing the success of negotiations. They can do this by anticipating that changes may occur and by managing them when they do.

The Problem

Changes that adversely affect negotiations can occur within either team, within either client's hierarchy, or even within outside groups involved in a settlement. Government environmental agencies are particularly prone to changes in both personnel (most commonly at the team level) and policy. The incidence of these changes varies from office to office and program to program. Changes tend to be most frequent in programs and offices most affected by statutory amendments, shifts in regulatory philosophy or approach, or staff increases or reductions (e.g., personnel attrition resulting from changes in program emphasis). New faces are especially likely to appear at the negotiating table when government leadership changes.

Government personnel or policy changes can have particularly severe effects on negotiations, and can greatly frustrate the regulated community. For instance, parties potentially liable for Superfund remedial action (potentially responsible parties, or PRPs) will experience a variety of difficulties when faced with a series of three on-scene coordinators (OSCs) during an 18-month negotiation with EPA over a remedial plan. Each OSC will need time and assistance to become familiar enough with the site to deal with its remediation. Each is apt to approach the problem with somewhat different assumptions, remedial preferences, and information needs. The resulting prevarication over remedial methods and the expense of new or repeated information gathering may convince the PRPs that EPA is less than zealous in its desire either to remedy the site or to do so without subjecting them to unnecessary expense. In turn, this perception will make the PRPs less willing to deal with EPA, and it will become harder for either party to manage the other. Thus, the adverse impacts of personnel changes on negotiations can delay site cleanup, possibly to the detriment of the environment and the public.

The greater the changes and the later they occur in the negotiation process, the more disruptive they can be. For example, if parties are close to settling on removal of hazardous waste to a specially constructed landfill, the settlement is apt to break down if a last-minute policy change requires that landfill cleanups be accompanied by bonds to guarantee perpetual care, or if a new OSC insists on fundamental design alterations. Either change could completely alter the PRPs' assumptions regarding the remedy's cost and desirability relative to other alternatives. Either could cause them to question whether EPA was operating in good faith, had any idea what it wanted, or was capable of final agreement on anything. EPA negotiators who sincerely want the matter settled and the site cleaned up may be just as frustrated with the change and resulting delay.

While personnel and policy changes may be particularly common—and, to the regulated community, particularly frustrating—in government, they are not unique to government. For example, the presidency of one hazardous waste management company recently changed hands three times in as many years, with each change bringing about its own brand of reorganization. Indeed, such changes are natural phenomena of large organizations. Negotiators therefore should not feel that they are the only ones whose teams and client hierarchies are beset with changing faces and policies. Moreover, they should remember that the very changes that are causing problems for them are probably frustrating their opponents as well.

Some Solutions

Proper management by both sides can sometimes avoid, and can frequently ameliorate, the difficulties caused by changing faces and policies. Even proper management by only one side can help.

Care in selecting team members may mitigate the problem of changing faces. The team leader should make sure from the start that team members will be there for the duration. If a member is to be transferred to another position, the leader should negotiate with the client hierarchy to assign another member for whom continuity is no problem, or to define the new job to include completing the negotiation. If a change in team members is unavoidable, the leader at the very least should assure that the outgoing member thoroughly briefs the new member. The team should also get the new member's agreement to accept and act consistently with what the team has done to date, to avoid replowing the same ground two or three times. If you anticipate changing faces on the other side, you can negotiate with it to take similar measures.

The effects of a policy change can be blunted if the potential change is spotted early enough. Perhaps the change can be delayed for a short period to accommodate a settlement, or worded to exclude negotiations in progress. Either option gives the team controlling the policy a lever to force a quick and favorable settlement. At the very least, a team should know of impending policy changes on its side and keep the other side informed of their timing and likely impact. This should speed the negotiations and avoid the embarrassment of having to restructure a settlement to avoid or accommodate an eleventh-hour policy change.

Chapter 7: Conclusion

Although negotiation is an art of its own, it has much in common with other types of interpersonal dynamics. Indeed, many of the thousands of everyday personal and professional interactions that involve give and take among people could be called negotiations. Therefore, if you are a novice negotiator, remember that many of the behaviors and attitudes appropriate to other situations to which you may be more accustomed are also appropriate to negotiation. Many of these behaviors and attitudes are simply applications of common sense.

This monograph has emphasized the importance of managing and being prepared for every step of a negotiation. Although these demands may seem heavy, remember that any successful process, from manufacturing to politics, requires management and preparation. If you think of negotiation as just another complex process in which you want to succeed, the need for management and preparation will seem natural.

The more specific types of action that are critical to success in negotiation are also common to other interactions. For example, you must know what you want, what you are willing to exchange for it, and what risks you are willing to take to get it. You must know what people and organizations are relevant to your situation, so that you don't make a deal with one person or faction only to get sandbagged by another. You must understand the other people you are dealing with as well as possible, so that you know how to motivate them. Your team must be coordinated, have clear leadership, and maintain a united front.

The attitudes you bring to a negotiation are also vitally important. Again, your experience with the attitudes appropriate to other interactions will be helpful. The basic ideas are simple. Keep calm and in control of yourself and the situation. Be firm about what you need, but flexible and open-minded about everything else. Don't worry about the lack of hard and fast rules. Write your own rules, stay light on your feet, and take advantage of unexpected developments. Play fair; everyone involved, including your opponents, must be able to trust you. Maintain a positive, confident attitude: A negotiation is a challenge that can benefit your professional development as well as your employer's interests.

Finally, as we mentioned at the beginning of this monograph, you can become an expert negotiator only if you practice. We strongly recommend the approaches and techniques we've discussed, but they are only the basics, like recipes in a cookbook. You have to work with them, experiment with the process, and develop your own natural style. Hopefully, you will come to find negotiation personally as well as professionally rewarding.

Appendix A: Time-Line Management In Negotiations

This Appendix is adapted with permission from material provided by:

American Arbitration
Association
140 West 51st Street
New York, NY 10020

(212) 484-4000

Office of National Affairs
American Arbitration
Association
1730 Rhode Island Avenue, N.W.
Suite 909
Washington, DC 20817

(202) 331-7073

I. PREPARATION PHASE

A. TASKS

1. Organize Preparation Phase
    a. Establish communications with hierarchy; identify communication channels to use throughout negotiation process
    b. Determine hierarchy's needs and goals
    c. Begin internal negotiations to influence goals and strategies
    d. Lower hierarchy's expectations
    e. Determine timeline for preparation phase, considering:
        i. ultimate bargaining deadline
        ii. personnel availability
        iii. resource availability
    f. Determine limits of team's authority
    g. Establish team operating procedures

2. Develop Team
    a. Establish communications within team
    b. Conduct team-building exercises
    c. Educate team members about different styles of thinking
    d. Determine each member's strengths and roles. Possible roles include:
        i. substantive expert
        ii. procedural expert
        iii. leader/facilitator
        iv. spokesperson
        v. media expert
        vi. corridor lobbyist
        vii. recordkeeper/designated listener/observer
        viii. editor/language expert
        ix. numbers expert
    e. Train team in negotiation process
    f. Lower expectations of team members
    g. Balance stabilizers and destabilizers
    h. Assign preparation phase tasks to each member

3. Gather Information and Identify Data Needs
    a. For your side's position

b. For other side's position
c. Identify external consultants and resources
d. Identify options to negotiation (e.g., arbitration, litigation)
e. Identify members of other team, and determine:
    i. their relationship with their hierarchy
    ii. their hierarchy's needs

4. Analyze Past Negotiations and Implementation of Past Agreements
    a. Review past negotiations of both teams
    b. Assess past negotiations, asking:
        i. did team achieve what it sought?
        ii. what procedures did it use?
        iii. what were strengths and weaknesses of past negotiations?
    c. Assess implementation of past agreements, asking:
        i. what items were difficult for us to comply with?
        ii. what items were difficult for other side to comply with?

5. Identify Issues
    a. Determine negotiable and non-negotiable items
    b. Determine "throw-away" items
    c. Determine likely sticking points

6. Identify All Interested and Affected Parties
    a. Perform public relations activities
    b. Build outside alliances
    c. Educate interested parties:
        i. in negotiation process
        ii. about team's goals
        iii. about anticipated difficulties
        iv. to lower expectations
        v. to avoid sabotage

7. Set Goals, Priorities, and Strategies
    a. Identify possible bargaining outcomes
    b. Set bottom line

c. Establish opening position
d. Develop strategy ("roadmap"), including:
    i. what you want to accomplish
    ii. signposts
    iii. desired timing
e. Determine real and announced deadlines
f. Plan for contingencies
g. Anticipate and analyze other team's demands
h. Prepare response to other team's anticipated opening position
i. Reach consensus within team
j. Obtain hierarchy commitment to bottom line

8. Ensure Availability of Administrative Support
    a. Clerical support
    b. Technical support
    c. Equipment
    d. Security

9. Arrange First Meeting of Phase II
    a. Create opportunities for informal, pre-negotiation meetings with other team to:
        i. avoid surprises
        ii. establish relationship
        iii. share information (if both sides so desire)
    b. Determine, with other team, basic conditions of first meeting, including:
        i. time
        ii. place
        iii. who will attend
        iv. whether meeting will be open or closed

B. POTENTIAL PROBLEMS (AND SOME SOLUTIONS)

1. Hierarchy gives team too little authority or gives unclear or changing instructions
    - Be flexible
    - Create doubts in hierarchy's mind

2. Team members have inconsistent goals
    - Use consensus decisionmaking techniques

3. Team or hierarchy lacks experience or continuity
   - Consider experience and continuity when selecting team
   - Conduct training and education

4. Other work or responsibilities create distractions
   - Manage time
   - Delegate

5. Lack of procedure causes confusion
   - Get ground rules and strategy in force early

6. Goals change continuously because of changing input from:
   - Public—do public relations work
   - Hierarchy—improve communications
   - Economic climate—improve costing techniques

II. ACTIVE MEETING PHASE

A. TASKS

1. Negotiate Procedural Issues
   a. Introduce team members
   b. Make seating arrangements
   c. Set agenda for current meeting
   d. Set times and places for subsequent meetings
   e. Determine ground rules for negotiation
   f. Determine which team presents opening position first
   g. Establish how to release information to media and public

2. Maintain Communication with Hierarchy
   a. Avoid surprises
   b. Lower expectations
   c. Create doubts as to viability of its positions
   d. Maintain clear line of authority
   e. Assess progress of negotiations
   f. Constantly restate goals

3. Manage Bargaining Process
   a. Distribute written summaries of previous meetings

b. Build trust; avoid promises or compromises you can't deliver
c. Prepare for possible mediation, litigation, or other alternatives
d. Avoid surprising other team
e. Create doubts as to viability of other team's positions
f. Lower expectations
g. Isolate stumbling blocks, bypass obstacles—go on to other items
h. Don't let team members talk out of turn or express disagreement at the table
i. List concerns of both sides
j. Rank priorities of both sides
k. Avoid unduly pressuring other team
l. Maintain physical and emotional edge (stamina, morale, and confidence) by taking breaks, getting "change of scene," and caucusing
m. Maintain communication with experts (if they are not at the table)
n. Listen!
o. Constantly frame questions regarding other team's proposals
p. Remain faithful to goals
q. Keep negotiations on track
r. Maintain tactical flexibility; remain open to new possibilities
s. Use "If ... Then ...." statements
t. Identify allies on other team
u. Identify opponents on other team and design specific responses to create doubt in their minds
v. Identify perceptions and assumptions underlying other team's positions
w. Don't let negotiations move too quickly or get bogged down.
x. Take notes on both sides' evolving positions
y. Clarify: constantly restate all agreements so far, and constantly paraphase other team's statements and positions
z. Take time to explain positions thoroughly

4. Accomplish Basic Tasks

a. Determine if and when closure might be reached
b. Exchange proposals and responses

c. Exchange information
d. Educate other team
e. Facilitate good working relationship by having both sides air feelings on items not to be negotiated

5. Caucus
    a. Maintain sight of goals by constantly restating them
    b. Create doubts in team members' minds
    c. Lower expectations
    d. Plan how to educate other team
    e. Analyze and react to other side's proposals
    f. Assess other side's reactions to your proposals
    g. Control internal tensions
    h. Plan strategies
    i. Control stabilizers and destabilizers

6. Manage Side-Bar Meetings
    a. Be honest, be yourself
    b. Don't surprise own team members—don't commit without first talking with them

7. Prepare for Closing Phase
    a. Establish timing and tactics for approaching Closing Phase
    b. Avoid pushing for closure prematurely
    c. Determine format of agreement

B. POTENTIAL PROBLEMS (AND SOME SOLUTIONS)

1. Other team surprises you
    - Prepare
    - Caucus

2. Other team is "un-psychable" (unreadable)
    - Have "walk-in-the-woods" session (informal, relaxed, private meeting)
    - Use series of true/false or yes/no questions

3. Number of issues grows
    - Use four "ings": clustering, dropping, giving, linking

4. Other side changes positions or lacks preparation
   - Be patient
   - Suggest caucus
5. Other side is inflexible
   - Suggest mediation
6. Communication with hierarchy is poor; hierarchy changes goals or instructions or limits team's authority
   - Re-educate
   - Re-focus
7. Team lacks discipline; destabilizers work against agreement
   - Create doubts
   - Use peer pressure
   - Confront
   - Replace
8. Other side feels its needs are not being addressed
   - Listen and ask questions
   - Hold side-bar meeting between chief spokespersons
9. Hierarchy's posturing for public opinion undercuts team's strategy
   - Use outside pressure (alliances with interest groups)
10. Information is leaked
    - Improve security
11. Teams cannot agree on ground rules
    - Hold side-bar meeting between chief spokespersons
    - Group those items teams can agree on
    - Compromise
12. Both sides have high expectations
    - Identify assumptions and perceptions
    - Frame questions to seed doubt
13. Other side has misperceptions
    - Present facts, data analyses, cost analyses

14. Teams do not listen to each other
    - Build trust
    - Be consistent and fair
    - Ask questions of other team and (in caucus) of own team

15. Team has difficulty maintaining unity of purpose and approach, either within itself or with hierarchy
    - Conduct ongoing communications

III. CLOSING PHASE

A. TASKS

1. Maintain Control as "Horse-Trading" Accelerates
   a. Identify and prioritize major unresolved issues
   b. Update your bottom line
   c. Assess likelihood of other team coming to agreement above your bottom line
   d. Analyze possible ramifications of any changes in positions
   e. Execute appropriate contingencies
   f. Maintain especially good (and quick) communication with hierarchy
   g. Continue public relations work
   h. Take careful, accurate notes
   i. Maintain united front
   j. Negotiate implementation mechanism for agreement
   k. Determine who will draft agreement
   l. Determine who will announce agreement, and how
   m. Ensure availability of administrative support

2. Come to Verbal Agreement
   a. Ensure that agreement is within position
   b. Confirm that all parties understand proposed agreement

3. Sell Agreement to All Concerned Parties
   a. Use other team's arguments to sell agreement to:
      i. destabilizers
      ii. hierarchy
      iii. constituents
      iv. outside interests

b. Get as much as possible for "losers"

4. Draft Agreement
   a. Allow opportunity for comment and revision
   b. Check every draft with team in caucus
   c. Reconfirm with experts and data base
   d. Reconfirm with hierarchy
   e. Reconfirm terms and language with other team

5. Close
   a. Sign agreement
   b. Observe any traditional protocol
   c. Publicize agreement, if appropriate
   d. Celebrate

B. POTENTIAL PROBLEMS (AND SOME SOLUTIONS)

1. Destabilizers make last-ditch efforts to prevent agreement
   - Educate as to cost of not closing

2. Other side attempts to re-open settled issues or to introduce new issues
   - Establish ground rules preventing introduction of new issues after designated cut-off

3. Stabilizers are too anxious to close
   - Remind them of wishes of constituents and hierarchy

4. Agreement goes beyond position acceptable to constituents or hierarchy
   - Consult with constituents or hierarchy
   - Hold side-bar meeting

5. Change in external factors makes agreement untenable
   - Bring in mediator

6. One side gets ratification, other side does not
   - Establish dispute settlement mechanism

7. Hierarchy enters negotiation
   - Get hierarchies together (if educated and experienced in negotiation process)

8. Team factions reach separate agreements
   - Control own team

9. Hierarchy continues to insist on unrealistic goals
   - Generate pressure on hierarchy to accept agreement

10. Time is a constraint
    - Identify individuals authorized to make decisions at critical times

11. Team spirit breaks down
    - Brief team members periodically as to generalities and details

12. Negotiations over agreement language continue after table negotiations end
    - Write language as items are agreed to

13. There are too many layers of authority in negotiation
    - Grant chief spokesperson more authority

Appendix B: Dispute Resolution Bibliography

Negotiation

Attorney's Guide to Negotiations. Springfield: Illinois Inst. for Continuing Legal Education, 1979.

Baer, H., & A. Broder. *How to Prepare and Negotiate Cases for Settlement*. New York: Law-Arts Publishers, 1973.

Bazerman, Max H., & Roy J. Lewicki, eds. *Negotiating in Organizations*. Beverly Hills: Sage Publications, 1983.

Beckmann, Neal W. *Negotiations: Principles and Techniques*. Lexington, Mass.: D.C. Health & Co., 1977.

Bellow, G., & B. Moulton. *Negotiation*. Mineola, N.Y.: Foundation Press, 1978.

Brown, L., & E. Dauer, *Planning by Lawyers*. Mineola, N.Y.: Foundation Press, 1978.

Calero, Henry H. *Winning the Negotiation*. New York: Hawthorn Books, 1980.

Claire, William H., III. "Winning Through Negotiation." 49 *Planning* 18-19 (July-Aug. 1983).

Cohen, Herb. *You Can Negotiate Anything*. Secaucus, N.J.: Lyle Stuart, 1980.

Colosi, Thomas R. "Negotiating For Profit." *The Insurance Field*, June 1984, 20, 43-46.

________. "Negotiation in the Public and Private Sectors: A Core Model." 27 *American Behavioral Scientist* 229-253 (Nov.-Dec. 1983).

________. "The Iceberg Principle: Secrecy in Negotiation." In *Perspectives on Negotiation*, edited by Diane B. Bendahmane & John W. McDonald, Jr., 243-61. Washington, D.C.: Foreign Services Research Center, U.S. Dep't of State, 1986.

________ & Arthur Eliot Berkeley. *Collective Bargaining: How It Works and Why*. New York: American Arbitration Association, 1986.

________ & Gregory A. Joseph. *Negotiating the Rules for Debate*. New York: American Arbitration Association, 1984.

Coulson, Robert. *How to Stay Out of Court*. 2d ed. New York: American Arbitration Association, 1984.

________. "Lawyers at Bargaining Table." *New York Law Journal*, Aug. 8, 1984, 1.

Davis, Tom H. "Settlement Negotiations." *Trial*, July 1983, 82-85, 120.

Dunlop, John T. *Dispute Resolution: Negotiation and Consensus Building*. Dover, Mass.: Auburn House Publishing, 1984.

Edwards, Harry T., & James J. White, eds. *The Lawyer as Negotiator: Problems, Readings and Materials*. St. Paul: West Publishing, 1976.

Eisenberg, Melvin Aron. "Private Ordering Through Negotiation: Dispute Settlement and Rulemaking." 89 *Harvard Law Rev.* 637-81 (Feb. 1976).

Fisher, Roger, & William Ury. *Getting to Yes*. Boston: Houghton Mifflin Co., 1981.

Goffman, E. *Strategic Interaction*. Philadelphia: University of Pennsylvania Press, 1969.

Hall, Joan. "Negotiation: Dispute Resolution As An Effective Alternative to Trial." 6 *American Journal of Trial Advocacy* 481-84 (Spring 1983).

Hawver, Dennis A. "Plan Before Negotiating . . . and Increase Your Power Of Persuasion." 73 *Management Rev.* 46-48 (Feb. 1984).

Haydock, Roger S. *Negotiation Practice*. New York: John Wiley & Sons, 1984.

Heller, Deborah, & David E. Berlew. "Negotiation Skills: Tools for Professional & Personal Success." 3 *Legal Administrator* 18-21 (Summer 1984).

Herman, P.J. *Better Settlements Through Leverage*. New York: Aqueduct Books, 1965.

Hunsaker, Johanna S., Phillip L. Hunsaker, & Nancy Chase. "Guidelines For Productive Negotiating Relationships." *Personnel Administrator*, Mar. 1982, 37-40, 88.

Illich, J. *The Art and Skill of Successful Negotiation*. Englewood Cliffs, N.J.: Prentice-Hall, 1973.

Jacobs, Bruce A. "Don't Take 'No' for an Answer." *Industry Week*, Jan. 26, 1981, 38-42.

Johnston, Robert W. "Negotiation Strategies: Different Strokes for Different Folks." *Personnel*, Mar.-Apr. 1982, 36-44.

Karrass, C. *The Negotiation Game*. New York: World Publishing, 1973.

________. *Give and Take*. New York: Thomas Crowell Co., 1974.

Kuechle, David. "The Art of Negotiation—An Essential Management Skill." *Business Quarterly*, Oct. 1982, 9-22 (Special Supp.)

Lax, David A., & James K. Sebenius. *Manager as Negotiator*. New York: Macmillan Co., Free Press, 1986.

Lewicki, Roy J., & Joseph A. Litterer. *Negotiation*. Homewood, Ill: Richard D. Irwin, 1985.

MacDougall, Donald J. "Introduction to Negotiation Theory." 58 *Law Inst. Journal* 1434-36 (Dec. 1984).

Main, Jeremy. "How to be a Better Negotiator." *Fortune*, Sept. 19, 1983, 141-46.

Miller, Ronald L. "Preparations For Negotiations." *Personnel Journal*, Jan. 1978, 36-39, 44.

Moberly, Robert F. "A Pedagogy For Negotiation." 34 *Journal of Legal Education* 315-25 (June 1984).

Nierenberg, Gerard I. *The Art of Negotiating*. New York: Simon & Schuster, 1968.

________. *Fundamentals of Negotiating*. New York: Hawthorn Books, 1973.

Nierenberg, Gerard I. *The Art of Negotiating*. New York: Simon & Schuster, 1968.

Raiffa, Howard. *The Art & Science of Negotiation*. Cambridge: Harvard University Press, 1982.

Rivkin, Malcolm D. "Principles of Negotiated Developments." *Envtl. Comment*, Nov. 1981, 4-6.

Schoenfeld, Mark K. "Strategies and Techniques for Successful Negotiations." 69 *American Bar Association Journal* 1226-30 (Sept. 1983).

________ & Rick M. Schoenfeld. *Legal Negotiation*. New York: McGraw-Hill, 1988.

Seltz, D., & A. Modica. *Negotiate Your Way to Success*. New York: Berkeley Publishing, 1981.

Susskind, Lawrence, & Jeffrey Z. Rubin, eds. "Negotiation: Behavioral Perspectives." 27 *American Behavioral Scientist* 131 (Nov.-Dec. 1983).

Swartz, Herbert. "Structured Negotiations Save Time, Money and Blood Pressure." *Electronic Business*, June 1984, 72, 74.

Ways, Max. "The Virtues, Dangers, and Limits of Negotiation." *Fortune*, Jan. 15, 1979, 86-90.

Wenke, Robert A. *The Art of Negotiation For Lawyers*. Long Beach, Cal.: Richter Publications, 1985.

Whitney, Gary G. "Before You Negotiate: Get Your Act Together." *Personnel*, July-Aug. 1982, 13-26.

Williams, R. *Effective Legal Negotiation*. Minneapolis: National Practice Institute, 1979.

Williams, Gerald R. *Legal Negotiation and Settlement*. St. Paul: West Publishing, 1983.

Williams, Gerald R. "Using Simulation Exercises for Negotiation and Other Dispute Resolution Courses." 34 *Journal of Legal Education* 307-14 (June 1984).

Zartman, I. William, & Maureen R. Berman. *The Practical Negotiator*. New Haven: Yale University Press, 1982.

Negotiation Ethics

Hazard, G. "The Lawyer's Obligation to be Trustworthy when Dealing with Opposing Parties." 33 *So. Car. Law Rev.* 181 (1981).

King, E., & D. Sears. "The Ethical Aspect of Compromise Settlement and Arbitration." 1952 *Rocky Mtn. Law Rev.* 454-62.

Rubin, A. "A Causerie on Lawyers' Ethics in Negotiation." 1975 *Louisiana Law Rev.* 577-93.

Shaffer, T. "Negotiation Ethics: A Report to Cartaphila." *Litigation*, Winter 1981, 37.

White, J. "Machiavelli and the Bar: Ethical Limitations on Lying in Negotiation." 1980 American Bar Foundation Research Journal 926.

Environmental Dispute Resolution

American Arbitration Association & Clark-McGlennon Associates. *Environmental Conflict Management:* New York: American Arbitration Association, 1981.

Amy, Douglas J. "The Politics of Environmental Mediation." 11 *Ecology Law Quarterly* 1-19 (1983).

Anderson, Frederick R. "Negotiation and Informal Agency Action: The Case of Superfund." 85 *Duke Law Journal* 261-380 (Apr. 1985).

Bacow, Lawrence S., & Michael Wheeler. *Environmental Dispute Resolution*. New York: Plenum Press, 1984.

Baldwin, Pamela. *Environmental Mediation: An Effective Alternative*? Report of Conference Held in Reston, Virginia, Jan. 11-13, 1978. Palo Alto: RESOLVE, Center for Envtl. Conflict Resolution, 1978.

Bellman, Howard S., Cynthia Sampson, & Gerald W. Cormick. *Using Mediation When Siting Hazardous Waste Management Facilities: A Handbook*. Washington, D.C.: U.S. Envtl. Protection Agency, 1982.

Bingham, Gail. *Resolving Environmental Disputes: A Decade of Experience*. Washington, D.C.: Conservation Foundation, 1986.

________ & Leah V. Haygood. "Environmental Dispute Resolution: The First Ten Years." 41 *Arbitration Journal* 3-14 (Dec. 1986).

Busterud, John. "Mediation: The State of the Art." 2 *The Envtl. Professional* 34-39 (1980).

Carnduff, Susan B. "Environmental Mediation in a Federal Agency." In *Environmental Conflict Management*, edited by Philip A. Marcus & Wendy M. Emrich, 48-55. Washington, D.C.: Council on Envtl. Quality and U.S. Dep't of Interior, 1981.

Clark-McGlennon Associates & American Arbitration Association. *Developing Methods for Environmental and Energy Dispute Settlement: Final Report*. Charlottesville: University of Virginia Inst. for Envtl. Negotiation, 1982.

Cormick, Gerald W. "Mediating Environmental Controversies: Perspectives and First Experience." 2 *Earth Law Journal* 215-24 (Aug. 1976).

Cormick, Gerald W. "How and When Should You Mediate Natural Resource Disputes?" Paper presented at Alternatives to Litigation Seminar, Washington State Bar Association, July 26, 1985 (available from Mediation Institute, Seattle, Wash.).

________. "Mediating Environmental Disputes." 10 *Journal of Intergroup Relations* 3-10 (Summer 1982).

________. "The Myth, the Reality, and the Future of Environmental Mediation." 24 *Environment* 14-17 (Sept. 1982).

________. "The 'Theory' and Practice of Environmental Mediation." 2 *The Envtl. Professional* 24-33 (1980).

________ & Leota K. Patton. "Environmental Mediation: Defining the Process through Experience." Paper prepared for AAAS Symposium on Envtl. Mediation Cases, Denver, Colorado, Feb. 1970. Seattle: Office of Envtl. Mediation, Inst. for Envtl. Studies, 1977.

Dinkins, Carol E. "Shall We Fight Or Will We Finish: Environmental Dispute Resolution in a Litigious Society." 14 *Envtl. Law Reporter* 10398-401 (Nov. 1984).

Galanter, Marc. " 'A Settlement Judge, Not a Trial Judge': Judicial Mediation in the United States." 12 *Journal of Law & Society* 1-18 (Spring 1985).

Harter, P.J. *Negotiating Regulations: A Cure for the Malaise?* Washington, D.C.: Administrative Conference of the United States, 1982.

Harter, P.J. *Negotiated Rulemaking: Some Preliminary Lessons.* Paper presented at Conservation Foundation Second National Conference on Environmental Dispute Resolution, Oct. 1, 1984.

Harter, P.J. "Regulatory Negotiation: The Experience So Far." *Resolve*, Winter 1984, 1.

Holznagel, Bernard. "Negotiation and Mediation: The Newest Approach to Hazardous Waste Facility Siting." 13 *Boston College Envtl. Affs. Law Rev.* 329-78 (Spring 1986).

Inst. for Envtl. Negotiation. *Not in My Back Yard: Community Reaction to Locally Unwanted Land Use.* Charlottesville: University of Virginia, 1985.

Jeffrey, Michael I. "Environmental Mediation: An Alternative Form of Dispute Resolution." *International Business Lawyer*, June 1984, 271-73.

Lake, Laura M., ed. *Environmental Mediation: The Search for Consensus.* Boulder: Westview Press, 1980.

McCarthy, Jane E. "Resolving Environmental Conflicts." 10 *Envtl. Sci. & Tech.* 40-43 (Jan. 1976).

________ & Alice Shorett. *Negotiating Settlements: A Guide to Environmental Mediation.* New York: American Arbitration Association, 1984.

McCrory, John P. "Environmental Mediation—Another Piece of the Puzzle." 6 *Vermont Law Rev.* 49-84 (Spring 1981).

McGuire, James E. "The Dilemma of Public Participation in Facility Siting Decisions and the Mediation Alternative." 9 *Seton Hall Legis. Journal* 467-73 (1985).

Mernitz, Scott. *Mediation of Environmental Disputes: A Sourcebook.* New York: Praeger, 1980.

Miller, Alan, & Wilf Cuff. "The Delphi Approach to the Mediation of Environmental Disputes." 10 *Envtl. Management* 321-30 (May 1986).

Moss, Larry E. "Beyond Conflict—The Art of Environmental Mediation." *Sierra*, Mar.-Apr. 1981, 40-45.

National Conference of State Legislatures. *Introduction to Environmental Conflict Management: A Legislative Perspective.* 1984.

Patton, Leah K. "Settling Environmental Disputes: The Experience with and Future of Environmental Mediation." 14 *Envtl. Law* 547-554 (Spring 1984).

Steinhart, Peter. "Talking it Over." *Audubon*, Jan. 1984, 8-13.

Stulberg, Joseph B. "The Theory and Practice of Mediation: A Reply to Professor Susskind." 6 *Vermont Law Rev.* 85-117 (Spring 1981).

Susskind, Lawrence. "Environmental Mediation and the Accountability Problem." 6 *Vermont Law Rev.* 1-47 (Spring 1981).

________, Lawrence Bacow, & Michael Wheeler, eds. *Resolving Environmental Regulatory Disputes.* Cambridge, Mass.: Schenkman Publishing Co., 1983.

________ & Scott McCreary. "Techniques for Resolving Coastal Resource Management Disputes Through Negotiation." *APA Journal* 365-74 (Summer 1985).

________ & Connie Ozawa. "Mediated Negotiation in the Public Sector: Media for Accountability and the Public Interest." In *Society of Professionals in Dispute Resolution: 1983 Proceedings, Eleventh Annual Conference* 32-50. Washington, D.C.: 1984.

Talbot, Allan R. *Settling Things: Six Case Studies in Environmental Mediation.* Washington, D.C.: Conservation Foundation, 1983.

Wald, Patricia M. "Negotiation of Environmental Disputes: A New Role for the Courts." *Columbia Journal of Envtl. Law* 1-33 (1985).

Watson, John L., & Luke J. Danielson. "Environmental Mediation." 15 *Natural Resources Lawyer* 687-723 (1983).

Weiner, Norman J. "Is Arbitration an Answer?" 15 *Natural Resources Lawyer* 449-56 (1982).

Mediation

American Arbitration Association. *Commercial Mediation Rules.* New York: American Arbitration Association, 1986.
Cohen, Richard, ed. *Mediation ... An Alternative That Works.* 2d ed. Salem, Mass.: District Court Dep't, Trial Court of Massachusetts, 1984.
Cooley, John W. "Arbitration vs. Mediation—It's Time to Settle the Differences." 66 *Chicago Bar Record* 204-21 (Jan.-Feb. 1985).
Folberg, Jay, & Alison Taylor. *Mediation: A Comprehensive Guide to Resolving Conflicts without Litigation.* San Francisco: Jossey-Bass, 1984.
Phillips, Barbara Ashley, & Anthony C. Piazza. "Using Mediation to Resolve Disputes." *California Lawyer*, Oct. 1983, 11-13.
Riskin, Leonard L. "Mediation and Lawyers." 43 *Ohio State Law Journal* 29-60 (1982).
Volpe, Maria R., & Thomas F. Christian, eds. *Problem Solving Through Mediation.* Washington, D.C.: Special Committee on Dispute Resolution, American Bar Association, 1983.

Arbitration

American Arbitration Association. *Commercial Arbitration Rules.* New York: American Arbitration Association, 1986.
Elkouri, Frank, & Edna Asper Elkouri. *How Arbitration Works.* 4th ed. Washington, D.C.: Bureau of National Affairs, 1985.
Goldberg, George. *A Lawyer's Guide to Commercial Arbitration.* 2d ed. Philadelphia: American Law Institute-American Bar Association Committee on Continuing Professional Education, 1983.
Peterson, Craig A., & Claire McCarthy. *Arbitration Strategy and Technique.* Charlottesville: Michie Co., 1984 & Supp. 1987.

Theory of Dispute Resolution

Bacharach, S., & Lawler, E. *Bargaining.* San Francisco: Jossey-Bass Publishers, 1981.
Bartos, O. *Process and Outcome of Negotiations.* New York: Columbia University Press, 1974.
Coddington, A. *Theories of the Bargaining Process.* Chicago: Aldine Publishing Co., 1968.
Cross, J. *The Economics of Bargaining.* New York: Basic Books, 1969.

Gulliver, P.H. *Disputes and Negotiations*. New York: Academic Press, 1979.

Nash, J. "The Bargaining Problem." 1950 *Econometrica* 155-62.

Pruitt, D. *Negotiation Behavior*. New York: Academic Press, 1981.

Rubin, J., & B. Brown. *The Social Psychology of Bargaining and Negotiation*. New York: Academic Press, 1975.

Schelling, T. *The Strategy of Conflict*. New York: Oxford Press, 1963.

Siegel, S., & L. Fouraker. *Bargaining and Group Decision Making*. New York: McGraw-Hill, 1965.

Young, O. *Bargaining*. Urbana: University of Illinois Press, 1975.